"Tears and laughter abound in this charming, interactive memoir. It's a book full of loss, love, and healing that will leave you wanting more from this debut author."

—**Suzanne Woods Fisher**, bestselling author of *Amish Peace: Simple Wisdom for a Complicated World*

"Shari Zook's story soars and sobs, punctuated by humor and wisdom. She reckons with, wrestles with, and worships the One who holds and heals the nations. Beware—just when you think you are safely on the sidelines, she will remember her reader and turn your way with a look of such insight and compassion that it may shatter—and then help restore—you."

—**Sheila Petre**, mother of nine and author of *Thirty Little Fingers*

"In *Peanut Butter and Dragon Wings*, Shari Zook invites her readers to pull up a comfy chair, take a deep breath, and join her in being honest about the challenges of living faithfully. She writes with authenticity and wisdom as she shares her personal experiences and the lessons learned from them. This book is a fresh wind of grace for weary women."

—**Gina Brenna Butz**, author of *Making Peace with Change: Navigating Life's Messy Transitions with Honesty and Grace*

D1275087

"Shari Zook says it best herself: 'This is not a book about self-care. This is a book about receiving the care that surrounds you.' *Peanut Butter and Dragon Wings* is not a cute mommy book about 'me time' and lattes. Shari's words—always honest, often harrowing—slice down to our darkest places and deepest needs. If she, a pastor's wife, loving mom, and competent woman, can hit the depths and find grace there, can reach out her hand and open her mouth to ask for help, then, God be praised, so can you and I."

—**Dorcas Smucker**, author of *Ordinary Days: Family Life in a Farmhouse*

"With refreshing honesty, Shari Zook drops the mask and shows us realness, brokenness, and pain. In candid, beautifully crafted stories, she bares her heart and shows us how we, too, can invite Jesus into our pain. I wept with her, and rejoiced as she continually points us to the God of grace. This book will bring hope to any woman who faces darkness and difficulty."

—**Faith Sommers**, author of *Prayers for a Simpler Life: Meditations from the Heart of a Mennonite Mother*

"Shari Zook has an ear for beautiful language and a gift for expressing emotional and spiritual concepts in concrete terms. I found myself laughing, crying, and understanding some of the difficult issues of life in new ways."

—**Lucinda Miller Kinsinger**, author of *Anything but Simple: My Life as a Mennonite*

PEANUT BUTTER

and

DRAGON WINGS

PEANUT BUTTER
and
DRAGON WINGS

A MOTHER'S SEARCH FOR GRACE

Shari Zook

HERALD PRESS

Harrisonburg, Virginia

Herald Press
PO Box 866, Harrisonburg, Virginia 22803
www.HeraldPress.com

Study guides are available for many Herald Press titles at www.HeraldPress.com.

PEANUT BUTTER AND DRAGON WINGS
© 2021 by Herald Press, Harrisonburg, Virginia 22803. 800-245-7894.
    All rights reserved.
Library of Congress Control Number: 2021933218
International Standard Book Number: 978-1-5138-0770-6 (paperback),
    978-1-5138-0771-3 (hardcover), 978-1-5138-0772-0 (ebook)
Printed in United States of America

Unless otherwise noted, Scripture quotations are from the ESV® Bible (*The Holy Bible, English Standard Version*®), copyright © 2001 by Crossway, a publishing ministry of Good News Publishers. Used by permission. All rights reserved.

Scripture quotations marked (KJV) are taken from the *King James Version*.

Scripture quotations marked (NIV) are taken from the *Holy Bible, New International Version*®, NIV®. Copyright © 1973, 1978, 1984, 2011 by Biblica, Inc.™ Used by permission of Zondervan. All rights reserved worldwide. www.zondervan.com The "NIV" and "New International Version" are trademarks registered in the United States Patent and Trademark Office by Biblica, Inc.™

Scripture quotations marked (NKJV) taken from the *New King James Version*®. Copyright © 1982 by Thomas Nelson, Inc. Used by permission. All rights reserved.

25 24 23 22 21   10 9 8 7 6 5 4 3 2 1

To my mom, who made it look easy,
and to my dad, who gave me paper.

Contents

Foreword

I am altruism run ragged. . . . I am human, and I need things."

I stared at Shari Zook's words, unable to move past the first page. I was hunched in the front seat of my twenty-year-old Subaru Legacy, in a strip mall parking lot where no one would know or notice or need me, biding time between a soul-crushing ministry meeting and a meeting with a congregant whose soul was being crushed. I had fielded a forlorn call from a beloved former foster child, whose spiraling behaviors had landed them in lockup, and from a social worker, who wondered if we could possibly . . . ? I had groceries to buy and a sermon to prepare, half a dozen foster and bio kids who needed me to be loving and attentive and present, a house and heart cluttered with messes that wore on me, but that I didn't have the time or energy to deal with. I had reached out to someone who hadn't reached back, and the sting of it made me wary. I was doing my best to care for everyone's needs, but who was taking care of me?

I am altruism run ragged. I am human, and I need things.

This is a book that tells the truth. It tells the truth about a lot of things, like the fact that we never stop yearning for a mother to swoop in and set everything right; that some children seem to emerge from the womb at odds with their parents' values; that girlfriends are a saving grace when men are being "outrageous" (which I assume is Mennonite for "doo-doo head," which is evangelical for something else, bless all our little hearts); that Good Christian Women™ and Relentless Christian Activists™ are two sides of the same coin, and neither are very good at saying no. But mostly, this book tells the truth about us human beings having limitations and needing things.

And before you even think about protesting that Jesus is all you need, and that you can do all things through Christ who strengthens you, consider these words from chapter 3: "Being a Jesus follower does not free me from needing. . . . Counting on him to make special allowances for me because I am a special human is not the way to walk with him. I am a normal human. I need the things normal humans need."

Ouch. Shari Zook may look like a sweet Mennonite pastor's wife, but she doesn't pull any punches!

"Messy grace" books have abounded in recent years, but this one is different. Having needs does not release us from responsibility; instead, it reminds us how much we need our brothers and sisters in Christ. Being stretched past our limits does not give us license to sin; rather, it is a painful reality in which we are invited to identify with our crucified Christ. Being depleted does not mean we should abandon the tasks God has set before us; it means we need to pick up our spoons, dip them in the peanut butter jar, and strengthen ourselves for the journey ahead.

Sometimes we need to say no. Sometimes we need rest, and medicine, and a good meal. But often what we need more than anything is to admit our need to others, and to allow them to minister to us.

We are human beings, and we need things.

Consider this book an invitation to pick up your spoon and dig into the sustenance that God has so generously provided through God's people.

—Jenny Rae Armstrong,
author of *From Risk to Resilience: How Empowering Young Women Can Change Everything*, pastor, and mother of four

Author's Note

The stories in this book are true to the best of my knowledge, but they are seen through my eyes. I offer my thanks to the many family members and friends who willingly permitted me to tell the stories we share, most especially my husband and my beloved children. I want to be a faithful steward of your hearts.

Introduction

Hello. How are you doing?

You're looking fabulous. Your kids are adorable, your husband is respected in the church, and you are rocking the good mom face. You've worked hard to get to this place in life. You have a position, and a voice that the people around you respect. They might tell you regularly how wonderful you are, what a great mother-cook-homemaker-employee-Sunday-school-teacher-friend. You have a lot to offer. Younger people look up to you, and older ones cluck their tongues fondly. *What a woman that girl is.* You've been saddled with a lot, but you're pulling it off.

You look great.

There's only a tiny crack, hon, and I can see in just enough to notice there's a hollow place. Are you okay in there, darling? It's okay—don't close it up, I didn't mean to scare you. A little fear is hanging out of it now. Maybe some need.

Oh, wait, I'm sorry. I'm looking in my mirror by mistake, and I thought it was you. I'm sorry.

My name is Shari Zook. I am a thirty-something-year-old who was basically born in a church pew. I'm a wife and mother and foster parent and pastor's wife and firefighter's wife. (Don't worry, that's all the same man. One husband is plenty.) I am a baker, a writer, an organizer, an herb grower, a volunteer. You can count on me to say yes, whether it's a quick meal for a new mom or a huge fundraiser for our Christian school. I am altruism run ragged. I am faith and doubt. I am confusion and clarity. I am bravery and fear. I am abundance and famine.

I am human, and I need things.

It takes me a long time to realize that.

I drive away from my house one day, reviewing my mental list of checkmarks. My house is tidy. My breakfast dishes are washed and stacked neatly. The house is reasonably clean. My older kids are all started on the day's rhythms and tasks. Three toddlers are strapped in their respective car seats behind me. The blond one is born to me, her eyes and pigtails radiant. The two with coconut oil smoothed into their hair, the two with the full and beautiful lips, I am driving to a visit with their birth parents. We are so clean and gorgeous we shine. It is nine o'clock in the morning, and we are ready. I might have yelled a little while chasing them around getting everybody dressed and combed, but we have pulled it off one more time. I have done it all.

Then my stomach rumbles, an unpleasant crumbling of my illusions.

You know what?

I have fed everyone but me.

I have no idea what to do with the hollow places in my body and heart. Isn't God supposed to fill those? Isn't taking care of everyone else enough? Most days, I don't remember why I am living the life I am, except it's what good people are supposed to do. But I always know, sure as heaven, that the moment I default, it's all going to come down. I try so hard to keep it together, to never let this telltale fissure show: *I am not the woman I want to be.*

The story I am about to tell you is a story of public performance and private inadequacy. My story is one of trying too hard to be the person who doesn't need. It's a story of hunger, of questions that don't have answers, and of what happens when Jesus turns out to be a deity who does not keep my structures from collapsing. Who isn't as interested in preserving my reputation and autonomy as I am.

This is a story of hell, and of heaven.

I thought the path to holiness was by way of being the giver and the food bringer and the savior. Not asking. Doing without. (How sweet and sacrificial a mama, taking care of everyone but herself.) I thought Christianity was about maneuvering so I am always in the giving chair, the good guy, the passer-outer of freezer meals and communion bread. I thought that if I did this well enough, God would satisfy me and protect me.

I guess I will have to try harder.

I guess running on empty is par for the course.

I guess I will have to pretend it doesn't matter.

I guess if anyone's going to do it, it's me.

I guess love hurts.

I guess I will stop wanting.

This philosophy works for a few hours, but fails to reckon with a basic truth: Mama is going to die without food. Or more likely, Mama is going to hit up the cheap carbs at about eleven o'clock because she is *hungry* and nobody made sure she had what she needed.

It is perfectly possible to starve in your own exquisitely functional life while making sure everyone else has enough. It is perfectly possible to drain your relationship with God down to zero while pouring others the wine, passing it around in a beautiful cup. *Come, share the Lord.*

This is not another book about self-care. I tried self-care, and it was like trying to live off my own body fluids. There's only so much there. This is a book about cracking open my perfect facade and saying, *I am not quite the person you think I am. I need things. I sinned today. I am asking for something from you. I am beset with fear and I am inadequate and I am terrified of you finding this out. I need.*

Actually saying these words to other people.

Now you have raw panic on your face.

Oh, wait, that's me again. I still fight this posture, this standing in need.

The earth is full of resources I will never access if I stay closed up and immaculate. The redeemed community is rich with them. In this story I will share with you what I learned the hard way, twelve surprisingly uncomfortable ways to reach for grace.

This is not a book about self-care. This is a book about receiving the care that surrounds you.

Come with me?

1

Two Other Hands

*The Power of Facing the
Darkness Together*

———————

The Lord is my shepherd, I shall not have needs
He maketh me to be just fine, thank you, and I have it covered
What you said did not hurt me, and what you did does not
    make me angry
But I have a friend you could pray for, she is really having a
    hard time

The Lord is my shepherd, I shall not desire
I am content with the status quo, and to admit hunger would
    mean to become incomplete

I am perfect in spirit, I drag along a body till I leave this old
     world, and it obeys me better if I don't listen
God's way is best I will not murmur, hallelujah

The Lord is my shepherd, I shall not struggle
Those people out there do not have him, poor souls, but here
     in the fold we are good
And always put our best hoof forward. Our sins, if we had
     any, are under the blood
There is no looking back and we're never in mental turmoil,
     praise the Lord

The Lord is my shepherd, I shall not want
It's been a while since I heard his voice but my wool is still
     squeaky clean. When he says
He comforts me I'm not sure what that means. As far as I
     know I have peace with God
And my fellowman so I don't have any enemies. What does it
     mean to restore a soul?

Here is a philosophy I have developed for dealing with lions,
yellow lights, and hard truths: If you don't look into their
eyes, they can't get you.

What lion?

The world is full of needs, and this is how the Jesus-people
make a difference: they always be the good guys. There are
probably others who are sponges and takers and failures, may
God forgive them, but I am a giver, a contributor to society, a

pillar of the church, and a great mom. I am the one who takes in needy children. I am the one who never forgets to bring food to potluck. I am so squeaky clean I am hardly human, and I have learned that it is best this way. Christians who cannot pull off a hallelujah don't get far.

When I am a child, I attend a one-room school in the wilds of northern Minnesota. One day when I am about seven years old, I need to use the bathroom, so I hold up one finger until the teacher nods at me, and I leave the room, climb the stairs, and enter our little corner restroom. Some time later, it becomes apparent to me that the toilet paper roll is empty and needs changing. I stand and reach for a new roll, and in trying to get it onto the dispenser, my hands fumble and I drop the entire roll into the toilet. I stare in horror as unclean water soaks into the paper, swelling it larger. What am I to do? One doesn't just reach into a dirty toilet. Calling for help is unthinkable. What would they say to me?

So I finish and pull down my skirt and walk out of that bathroom. I step down the stairs to my desk and I pick up my pencil and I solve a math problem.

If you don't look into their eyes, they can't get you.

I am even more a child, only five years old, when my pastor father takes me on a thousand-mile trip to preach at several churches. He learns how to braid my hair for the occasion, and although my part is crooked some days, I am adorable and well behaved and we have a lot of fun together. While he preaches, I sit alone on an unfamiliar front pew and listen. One evening I begin to fidget. I need the bathroom (again) (already). Five years old. Growing more and more uncomfortable. I am sitting in a church pew with no one to tell my needs to. I am ashamed and starting to cry and I needa pee. My father watches me out of the corner of his eye, and presently interrupts his sermon to speak to our hostess, sitting in the congregation. *Would you please take my daughter to the restroom?*

My relief and shame mingle as I walk out past all those faces. Don't look into their eyes.

The next night, same church, second sermon, my nose begins to run. I sit on the wooden pew, not a tissue to be seen, my nose dripping. I sniffle and wipe it on my hands and it won't stop. I begin to cry again, silently, which doesn't dry up anything for sure. In the middle of his preaching, my father reaches into the back pocket of his suit pants where he always keeps it, takes out a folded white handkerchief, and tosses it to me, a perfect arc from pulpit to pew. It lands beside me, skidding on the smooth wood. Hallelujah.

Maybe this is when I start trying so hard.

I try to be a good daughter, sister, friend, wife, mother. The kind who doesn't need much, who can figure out a way to use a wooden bench to plug a runny nose, who can dig my own toilet paper out of the swamp or pretend it isn't drowning there. Who keeps the system going so things look good and no one is ashamed of me or humbled by my humanity. Who turns my angst inward and takes it out on no one but me. As long as I am the only one suffering, we are fine.

That is how I turn into a thirty-something-year-old woman who shines the light out into the world and holds the darkness in. I am a child and then I am an adult, trying to figure out how I got where I am, and when I started promising myself that I will never reveal needs in a way that inconveniences, obligates, or embarrasses other people. If I don't look at it, is it there? If I don't give it a name: depression: grief: marital pain: unbelief: is it real?

My needs grow as I grow, and by the time I am an adult they are so big I am afraid they will overcome me, and everyone else. Not to mention the needs of others, and how they come knocking harder and faster as I age, the enormous needs of a hurting world. I close my eyes and work like mad. I fix everything I can. I become as perfect as I can.

I don't want to look at the dark things in myself, because they do trauma to my self-image as a good, competent person. I don't want to look at the dark things in the world, because I am a small person and however holy I live, I cannot fix the problems of the universe. I cannot heal good people or change bad people. I cannot save the children who are dying from contaminated water in small villages. I can't even change my own bad habits, make one hair of my head white or black.

Lions and darkness and hard truths.

What is hiding there in the darkness?

What will happen when I shine the light into its eyes?

I am not one of the saints who thinks Jesus is fine with me no matter what. I am raised to understand that he is love and also justice. He wants his people good, and moving in the world. I know that holy living demands something of me, and I cannot quite pull it off. I invest heavily in the work of the kingdom because I love Jesus and I believe in him—and because what else is there? So I say yes by default, do all the things, sign up for the hard stuff that will break me, because I believe this is the way and I want to be his and I am called to make a change in the world alongside him.

I plan the picnic for forty people and I harvest food from the garden and I make it to all the appointments and I bake four cakes for the fundraiser and I arrange a playdate at a park and I babysit and I take my foster son to Pittsburgh for extensive dental work and I make supper for the new family in town and I teach Sunday school and I host a houseful of people for dinner after church.

In one week.

Then I lie in my bed in the darkness and I cry hopelessly, despairingly, desperately, because I don't remember why I did any of it. I am a woman who knows how to take care of everyone else, but I don't know who will take care of me.

I am a person and a woman and a foster parent and a pastor's wife and an Anabaptist, and I am afraid to look into the darkness because underneath the despair I am angry and it's not nice to be angry at God. These truths we hold to be self-evident: God is good, life is a battle, and pastors' wives have answers. But some days, I hold on to hope with my fingernails because if there's Someone out there, it doesn't seem like he's making any difference. I hope he's real, and I hope I am praying to the right one, because it would be a real bummer to get to heaven and find out I was wrong.

I am angry that he is not holding up his end of the bargain. He is supposed to care about me. He is supposed to care about healing this earth, more than I do. Is what I am doing making any difference? And why am I so empty?

I will follow the line of words, as Annie Dillard wrote, and I will place my hand on one word after the other, hand over hand, until I have made a path for myself out of this abyss.

I feel an absurd fear in doing so. Light shimmers from words, and what will it uncover? I would hope things like *faith* and *hope* and *understanding*, but maybe not. I feel an absurd fear, and I have to psych myself up for it with untraditional songs.

I am an Anabaptist and a pastor's wife and a foster parent and a woman and a person, and sometimes I find that the words of faith ring hollow, that its music slips over my head, too high, unreachable, because it says things like *My Jesus is so close and so real and I can feel him at every moment.*

And it says, *Nothing can ever threaten or trouble me.*

And it says, *Or if it does—Heaven! Hallelujah.*

Sometimes I need to hear the helpless angry percussion of old rock songs that say, *Just when you think you're getting the hang of life, it rises up and kicks you in the groin.*

And, *How will the universe have meaning now that you, my darling, are gone? You are gone. You are gone, gone. How will the universe have meaning? Now that you, my darling, are Gone.*

Sometimes bad things happen when you shine light into pain.

On the day I speak to my father's college class about my history of depression, my daughter throws up at school, one of my sons misbehaves all through math class, the other awakens with night terrors, and when I go to bed I am visited by a nightmare of my own.

I enter an old house, the one we lived in when my first son was born. Walking with me, his hand in mine, is my second son, my wild child, the one who has blown all my formulas. The one with whom I walked the cliff line of depression. In my dream this night, he is docile, his eyes wide and innocent.

Here was our kitchen, I say. *Here was Daddy and Mommy's bedroom. Here was our living room.*

Hand in hand, we step across the threshold. The picture window is enormous, staring blankly into the night outside. Something in the room feels unfamiliar, and I turn in confusion in time to see the exterior door swing eerily, forcefully inward. Beyond it is only darkness and an unseen presence, a living mass of palpable fear rushing into the room to get us.

I scream a timeless movie scream, locked into place, mouth wide in terror.

I have screamed this way in real life, when my soul is casting itself out and every drop in my mouth is blood.

The force seizes us, pulls us weightless through the door into the night, catches us into the air above the earth. We are rolled in hatred, heading for destruction, enmeshed in malicious, unmixed evil. Snowflakes swirl about us. I cling to my son's hand. I speak a prayer past the choking sensation in my mouth, each word an effort. One word after another. Hand over hand.

Jesus. Give me strength to bring my son back to the light.

And suddenly we are rejected by the evil. I feel myself shoved hard from the back, a deliberate denunciation—shoved clean out of the land of dreaming, and solidly into waking.

I lie frozen in my own bed, immobile with fear, my hands tucked under my chest. Waking, I feel the distinct pressure of two other hands in mine, nonphysical, invisible, but real. For uncounted heartbeats I lie breathing, quieting myself, feeling the pressure, warm and close. In my left hand is the hand of my precious son, retained, safe, brought by mercy through the darkness.

In the other is the hand of Christ.

Don't be afraid, honey, my husband says softly into my hair, when I have trailed him out of bed and told him all of it.

I don't think it's a picture of what's going to happen. I think it's a picture of what already did.

The reason I go on at all is because I think Jesus is here. The reason I must go on is because little people are depending on me. They need a hand to hold to. I need a hand to hold to. This is my confession: that I have tried my whole life to live so that I don't need his mercy.

I live a high-functioning life. I was raised for success. I can nail this mom thing and friendship thing and community servant thing. I can do it all.

Until I can't.

Until, inside, I come to the place where digging deeper and trying harder doesn't work, the place where I feel the rising panic of futility, floodwaters in the basement of my heart. I don't know what to do with my unmet need, my growing fear, my hidden loss and failure, and I'm terrified of letting anyone in. I don't know where to turn if underneath all the good things I begin to suspect that I am a really messed up person and that my soul has holes that cannot heal.

What is light but allowing others to see in?

The landscape of my heart is pretty scary, strewn with my hungers and sins in the twilight. The expectations of others lurk nearby. Deeper still are my fears about God. What if he is not who I think he is? Behind it all cringes Satan, that old liar, always afraid of coming to the light. His power is in hiding and shadowing, confusing the evil and the good, deceiving the heart.

Allow me to shine truth on him for one moment.

He is a bully and a coward. He wants to destroy, but lacks the courage (or permission) to go about it outright. He slinks and sneers and insinuates and twists. He plays shadow shows in the mind of evils he does not have the power to bring about. He works on my fear.

Only the devil takes a tiny grain of truth that I really need to hear and covers it up with a mountain of grains, a crushing, paralyzing weight of judgment. If he can, he'll bury me in condemnation. Failing that, he hopes that when I struggle panting out of the mound, I will reject the entire stack and walk away. He has successfully distracted me from the bit I needed: the still, small voice, the truth.

He agrees with God; and goes much, much further. The quiet truth I hear in my spirit is, *You need to ask for help.* And the lie, piling on hard and fast, says, *That's right. You need* HELP. *You are a nasty piece of baggage and everyone is going to find out and your cover will be blown. What an embarrassment you are. I can't even* BELIEVE *how much* HELP *you need.*

I shake myself out from beneath the weight and say NO. *I am in Jesus. I am forgiven and I am fine,* and I walk away. But when I do this, I miss the voice I needed to hear, which is still the truest truth underneath the lie. *You need to ask for help.*

Satan is a double-crosser and a cheap con. He's the only liar who can tell me opposite things simultaneously, and get me believing both. He says I am a terrible mother because I am too hard on my kids, and also because I am too easy on them. He says I am too despicable for words, and also that an important person in my position should be ashamed of myself for stooping so low. He says I am going to drown, and also that if I admit my weakness and lift my voice and reach out my arms for help, I will sink for sure. He says there is no one to assist me, and also that everyone is watching. *What will they think?*

The voice that says *No hope* is always from the darkness. *You are trapped* is not a phrase that ever crossed the lips of Jesus, nor *What will they think?*

The devil is a wolf trying to single out a single member of the antelope herd in order to bring it down. He is convinced down to his bones of what we humans are often unaware of, or unwilling to accept: that there is safety in the herd and that we are stronger together. He can't get at the Christian community unless we divide and isolate ourselves, or turn against each other.

Privately, he mixes a stiff personal attack (guilt, anxiety, failure, loss) with the conviction that we must face it alone. He berates us for our inadequacy, real or imagined, and then tells us never to share it with anyone. And we listen to him. We close ourselves into our perfect shells of light, and isolate ourselves from the resources that will heal us. This is the great tragedy of Christian womanhood in America.

Light is allowing others to see into my darkness.

My own insight is small, and it wobbles. But I am not alone. I reach for the light of the Holy Spirit, the light in the eyes of the body of Christ, his people who can call this evil what it is and reject it. With them I turn to face the things I fear: the messed-up world, the old fox, the broken places in my soul, and my utter inability to be what I want to be. I stand in the strength of a risen Jesus. I stand in the light. I stand in the center of my own life and name what I am.

> My name is Shari Zook. I am human, a body and a soul.
> I am flawed and messed up and trying too hard, conceited by my success and devastated by my failure and treasured every moment.

I do not have to be perfect to be wholeheartedly embraced by love.

I am not measured by my achievements and victories, but by the righteousness of Christ.

I need help. I am allowed to need, because none of my needs will overwhelm his grace. He is already preparing the people and situations I will encounter for my healing.

I can repent and change. I am forgiven, again and again and again. I am in Jesus, all of me.

I am called to his work, made worthy by his goodness.

I am not big enough to mess up the plans of God. They go on, with or without me.

I am surrounded by people who can help me, and people who need permission to face their own insufficiency.

I am never alone, never the only one.

I am made for communion with other humans. To turn from them is to shut out Christ.

I do not have to hide what he has made me, what I have made myself, what I am.

I am made for joy, for hope, for light, for love.

I am a child of the Most High God, created with tenderness, redeemed by grace, hallowed by the blood of Jesus.

I am willing to walk through the darkness to get to the light.

So I go to worship and put myself in another church pew because I am the pastor's wife and because it is the next thing and because I have the teacher's manual for Sunday school class. I cry there, and I still try to hide the tears and snot with my hands. I need help. I need permission to be honest about my needs and sins, my fears and failures. I need to know how to live in a world where there is an overwhelming amount of demands and too many of them are knocking at my own door.

I confess there are times I cannot find the hand of Christ, and I find him only when I reach for his people. I the child, and they the middleman.

They surround me with the voices of angels and they pray all around me. They sing in my ears. The songs say *Heaven, hallelujah*, but it's okay because it's not me singing. It's us. There is a newborn baby there, and a gray-haired layman reading the Word in a polo shirt, and a child in pigtails, and an insightful pastor I am in love with, and a friend who will ask how I am doing. They are called his body for a reason. Jesus dwelling still in flesh and skin. I can reach out and touch, can hold and be held.

I go to church because I need holiness to be a place where the givers can also receive, and the receivers can also give.

I go because I need the redeemed community to touch me and say, *Be healed*. None of us has any illusions that it will happen overnight. We're not a miracle healing kind of congregation. We're more like a do-what's-right-until-the-Lord-shows-up congregation. *Our faith has saved you. Go in peace.*

My people hold on to Jesus with one hand and me with the other.

My people hold on to faith with both hands. For me.

There are times when I cannot find my way to God myself, and I need someone else, the raw songs and the saints, to say the things. That is how I get through another day.

You probably don't believe me, but just a moment. Let me tell you how it all started.

1

LOOKING INSIDE

————

At the end of each chapter, I'd like to sit with you and Jesus a moment and be still, because I can talk until the cows come home about my life, but what you need may be an honest evaluation of your own. I invite you to take a brave look into your experiences and longings. This is your space to reflect, but I promise you that he is here. So am I.

1. Do you identify with my need to hide my struggles and desires? When did you start requiring yourself to be so strong?

2. Which words resonate with your current state of heart?

    JOY   INADEQUACY   NEEDINESS   STRENGTH
    FEAR   EXHAUSTION   DOUBT   HOPE
    COMPETENCE   PRETENDING   OTHER: _____

3. Place your hiding on a sliding scale, somewhere between *nervousness* about looking bad at one, and *straight up terror* at ten. Where are your particular places of fear?

1   2   3   4   5   6   7   8   9   10

4. Would you name some ways in which you are not the person you would like to be? (I told you this would take a bit of courage.)

5. Have you found the grace to shine light on these areas by allowing others to see in? If not, could you brainstorm for a moment about someone you could trust to look at a little part of it? We will go on together from there. A twinkle is still a light.

2

Cracked Eggs on White Carpet

The Freedom of Admitting Need

D one with the ponderous, the swollen, the out of breath, I

E ndure the aching groaning shriek of my body as it brings

L ife into a fallen world. A child is born this day.

I have never seen anyone so perfect. His

V ery tears sparkle with the light of a world I've seen only
in dreams, his wail is an

E cho of the holy child on his own arrival here.

R eaching to touch, to hold, to worship, my body and heart
are healed,

Y et the sword of our shared humanity, our loss, our love
pierces my heart.

One night when I am twenty-two years old, I stay up until one o'clock in the morning watching *Ben-Hur* with the good man I married, and when I go to bed my waters break and we end up in the new life unit bringing our first baby into the world, one week early.

Remind me, I whisper to my husband during transition, *not to do this again.* He reads John Grisham in between contractions until I make him stop. *We're in this together, you old coot, and I'm over here dying.*

When I hold my son, after twelve hours of a textbook labor and delivery, the world splits open and melts itself down over the three of us. Warm. Liquid. Remade. We are a mommy and a daddy. What I cannot fathom, more than anything, is that suddenly there is an extra person in the room. *A person.* From us.

I've never seen a child so intelligent and aware. When they place him in my arms, his big dark eyes latch onto mine and he stares deep into them, looking, blinking, figuring me out, listening to me baby-talk nonsense out of my mind. My son. What is time in those moments? The three of us must share half an hour of intimate, spellbinding focus, laughing, weeping. Our son.

We make it through our first full night in the hospital. I learn how to breastfeed. I struggle to change his first messy diaper while the nurse watches to make sure I can do it right. I dress him in enormous baggy newborn clothes, all seven perfect pounds of him, and we bring our baby home.

I know I'll be a good mom. I've spent nine months starry-eyed, great with child and ambition. Before that, twenty-odd years in training with kids. I am the second of seven siblings, the last of whom was born when I was sixteen. I am the daughter of two faith giants. My father counsels families on marriage and child training, and my mother birthed and raised a whole houseful without breaking a sweat. Babies are familiar to me, and children home turf: I am going to know exactly what to do.

But the next days and weeks are a different story, as my hormones begin their slow plummet, and I trail behind them like a limp kite tail straight into the pit of cluelessness. The canyon of inexperience? You can get lost down there. I know.

My mother comes to help me for a week, and when she packs her bags to leave again, inadequacy and fear congeal into a lump in my throat. I am so alone. My husband and I are both new to this neighborhood, and all extended family lives hours away.

How am I supposed to know how much milk my son is getting? And when he should start sleeping through the night? I pore over mothering books, hoping against hope I am not messing him up. Is it okay if I rock him to sleep? Or is that taboo? It depends which book I read. How many feedings a day? What am I supposed to do about cradle cap? Is it normal for his belly button to look like that? Oh my stars.

Is it okay if I dissolve into tears at two in the morning when he blows through three diapers in a row and is screaming to nurse and I am so tired I can't see straight and know I can't do this anymore, or will that sour my milk and give him a bellyache?

I am not joking. Thanks to some coaching from a beloved woman I won't mention who raised seven without turning a hair, I believe the latter for many months, and spend way too much time tying myself up in knots so I won't be stressed out so tension will not be communicated into my breastmilk, which apparently has ears in the cornfield and sentinels in the psyche. (This is obviously super relaxing information.) Every time my baby gets a little squirmy, she who shall not be named says gently, *Were you uptight when you nursed him?* and I say, *Uh, I don't think so . . . No more than usual.*

HELLO.

YES.

I AM A FIRST-TIME MOTHER AND I AM UPTIGHT.

IF YOU SAY THE WRONG THING, I WILL FIRST GNAW YOUR HEAD OFF AND THEN BURST INTO REPENTANT TEARS AND THEN GIGGLE HELPLESSLY OVER YOUR CORPSE.

Someday when I am brave, I will tell her she is wrong, and she will apologize, and we will all be good. Of course, she may be right. She is smarter than I am. But for all practical purposes, I need to believe she is wrong in this. It helps.

The mothering mantle lies heavy on my shoulders. Of course I know about babies. What I don't know about is motherhood. There has always been someone else to pass a child off to when I am bored or tired or in over my head. The Mom. What does it mean to be The Mom, and who is looking out for this child to make sure I do a good job? I assumed there'd be more training somehow, a heavenly cloak falling from the sky to show me what I am supposed to do. I have no secret wisdom and no confidence, and the job never ends so I can go home and chill.

Nothing prepares me for the solitude. The mind-numbing repetition of acts. The anxiety, the sense of impending dangers all around. I love him so much I am out of my head with loving.

Is it okay to leave him with Grandma for half an hour so I can get out of the house and go for a drive with my husband? One time in that first week, I do it, and am distressed to realize I have a nearly physical chain connecting me to my baby, tugging at my heart every moment I am gone. Is he okay? What if he needs me?

How do people carry this weight and survive?

I have trouble sleeping at night, because in the hum of the air conditioner I think I hear him crying. And then he is crying, and I have to get up with him. Again.

Oh, he is precious. He smells like sweet milk and baby lotion, and his hair is perfect, and his skin.

If only I knew what I was doing, and if only I could get some real sleep.

I go to a six-week check-up at the pediatrician and she says, *How are you doing?* I say, *I am doing fine, it's tricky getting used to mothering but it's coming. I'm eating okay, sleeping when I can. I'm okay. Yeah, I'm fine. Thank you.*

Anything to keep from cracking open to the darkness, because I know it will drown me.

The days and the nights creep by. I grow sore and cold, exhausted, ancient. I know my breasts will never be my own again, and I'll never cook a decent supper again, and my son will be newborn for a good fifteen years, at this rate. All the other moms seem to be doing fine, loving every minute. Some of them actually conceive again, on purpose, and look happy about it.

I will never say what I feel: I can't do this. I'm not going to make it. I wish he were someone else's baby so I could love him all I want but someone else would take responsibility for making sure he doesn't die. Is it okay that his dad doesn't show any interest in changing his diaper? Can I eat garlic bread, or will that make him spit up? Is he holding his head high enough during tummy time?

Oh my Lord.

Someday in the far distant future when I am brave and experienced (the far, far distant future), I will look back on that little mama and wish I could go back and put my arms around her.

Honey, relax. Let it all out, it's okay. Breathe.

Your baby will tell you what he needs. You can follow any method that works for the two of you, any book you want, but don't forget to give yourself grace. Mothering will never be a science; it's an art that you and your baby are crafting together. First times are always anxious. That's what loving is like.

Look at him. He's so healthy and so fine.

Relax.

Get out sometimes, and then come back quickly and love him up. Breathe in his skin. Look in his eyes. Laugh at yourself a little. Some days dress him up handsome, just for you. Other days, keep him in pajamas and stay in your own. Get some coffee and snuggle late into the morning.

Jesus made you his mommy, and that means you can do it—and when you can't, you can ask for the help that you need. You're doing fine, little mama.

Here is something I do not understand: Why don't we get more training for the hardest job of our lives? Why do we feel that we have to do it alone?

I have feelings that scare me. I have needs I don't know how to verbalize. I long for things I can't even identify. Sleep, primarily.

In Minnesota where I grew up, asking for things straight out is rude, an inconvenience or obligation to others. As often as possible, I keep a low profile and wait for someone to notice what I need. And therefore I find out the hard way that people are not good at mind reading. What is wrong with them?

I don't know how to ask, but I need someone to speak reassurance to me. I need grace for the child I am: so sheltered, so loved, that I have no idea how to be an adult. I need someone to put food on a plate and hand it to me, because the act of walking to the kitchen and preparing victuals and making twenty-nine tiny choices is too much. (Which yogurt am I hungry for? Eggs over medium or scrambled? Have the leftovers gone bad?) I need permission to lean on other moms who will walk with me. I need to know that the crushing responsibility will lighten. I need to know that I might want more kids someday. And that if I don't, it will be okay. I need a few moments to take a shower without worrying that he'll cry. I need to be told I can do this.

To be honest, I also need medication for postpartum depression and anxiety, but I don't know what that is yet and I wouldn't admit it if I did. The only smooth and perfect shells I crack open, so hollow, so slight, are the ones I empty into a skillet, preparing my own breakfast. What will happen if I open up? I am not ready to find out.

When did it become taboo to admit who and where I am?

I never let on to my doctor, and it takes a full year for the darkness to gradually dissipate, as my hormones level out and I get the hang of my new role. I hold on until I realize I am myself again. I am smiling all over my face, and laughing without pain. I have a beloved son, a toddler boy who is smart and precocious and cheerful and mine. I am a mother, and relatively peaceful in my hard-won role, at last. I am even willing to think about more children.

Another year later, my second son comes along.

The second time around, I am not undone by his birth, and my postpartum wilting is much shorter. For this I give thanks. He is slightly fussier, but a decent baby with a good first year, on track with all his milestones. I love his little turned-up nose and his impish grin and his pudgy baby fat.

But when he turns one and starts walking, his throttle sticks, inexplicably, on Full Speed Ahead. If I put him at the top of a slide, he flings himself down headlong and comes up with blood on his face. If I set him on a sidewalk, he takes off toddling and never looks back. Ever. If I go upstairs, he heads for the kitchen, opens the fridge door, and starts dumping things.

We have a decorative table he loves to push over. We stand it up again. And again, until the day the glass top shatters. He digs in the brown sugar. He pours out everything he can find. He reaches across my plate to get my cup of milk and splash it onto my dinner. Beverages splatter the kitchen floor while we host guests in the living room. Jugs of cream from the fridge. All the bathwater splashed by the bowlful onto the bathroom floor. All his clothes out of the drawer. Canisters of sugar.

He bites his brother through the skin and throws apple slices and knocks books off shelves and flashes the darlingest blue-eyed smiles. He writes in crayon on my kitchen door, and in permanent marker on our library books and our carpet, in long lavish streaks. He drizzles breakfast syrup over everything in my dining room, and runs to me for snuggles. He grabs knives and strips leaves off African violets and pushes over floor lamps and drops his father's technological devices down the toilet.

He isn't even two years old yet.

I know about mothering now, kinda. But I am way beyond my depth.

One morning, I walk into the living room and find eggs everywhere. One is cracked onto the keys of the piano, another soaks into its wooden bench, and two more are smashed on my white living room carpet. My son has fetched them from the fridge and beat the tops with a wooden spoon for a while, then tossed them about. *Actually, I did this one,* my older son-with-a-conscience confesses. He is still shy of four himself, and up for a good time. *I didn't want to tell you but it looked so fun.*

Within days it is loose leaf tea on the floor, onion powder, Elmer's glue in generous streaks and puddles on the carpet. When my younger son doesn't like his consequences, he throws stuff at me and his brother: books, toys, a tennis ball, a plastic tea pot, a stepstool. He has deadly aim. Or he laughs. Or bites himself.

He is sensory and hyperactive and busy and charming and mischievous. He can be reckless and calculating and cruel. I must watch him constantly. The older he gets, the worse his compulsions become.

He is the kid who starts singing "B-I-N-G-O" at the top of his voice in Sunday morning church, right at the high point of his father's sermon. When I clap my hand over his mouth, he is furious. Shapes his fingers into a gun and pretends to shoot me.

When he turns three, I give birth to a baby daughter I desperately want to protect. He nicknames her Daisy, and touches her nose so tenderly with his finger (or bangs her on the head with his fist).

One day in January, we disassemble our Christmas decorations and he beats my blue porcelain angel with a white porcelain cherub until one of them crunches into pieces.

What?! I say.

I wanted to break it, he tells me. *First I rolled it back and forth, but when it didn't break, I hit it with this.*

Honey, I say tenderly, *if Mommy broke one of your treasures, my heart would be so sad. Why is your heart not sad to ruin one of Mommy's treasures?*

Because, he says, *it's just fun to see stuff break.*

We know he is sensory-driven, impulsive, extremely intelligent. But we have no idea what is going on in his mind. Why he won't respond to discipline, which we keep consistent. Why he is brilliant in learning academically, but unable to learn anything behaviorally.

When he is three years old, he begins sounding out words. At four, he reads his first chapter book and starts pecking out adorable emails in caps lock, zero punctuation. DEAR GRAMPA DO YOU NO THAT I LOVE YOU SO MUCH THAT I CKANT LOVE YOU NOT I MORE YOU ARE SO SPESHLL TO ME. (He asked how to spell *dear* and *are*.) DEAR JEAN ARE YOU WITH GRAMA AND ON YOUR WAY TO HER HUOS FER THE WEEKEND WITH ALL THE PEPLE IN YOUR FAMLY AND US I HOPE YOU GET BETER SOON I CAN MACKE A PICTER FER YOU IF THIS IS NOT UNUF. At five, he reads the unabridged *Wonderful Wizard of Oz*. I have no idea how much he is understanding, but he keeps stopping to tell me what chapter he is on and how many witches are left.

Oh, he's a honey. He is big and beautiful—the blondest and bluest—a sweetheart and a charmer. He loves stories and snuggles and animals of all kinds and *diggies*, his word for all construction equipment. He cooks with me, makes friends, talks up a storm.

He becomes violent when he is angry. Even happy, he has troubling disconnections in his mind, allowing him to say and do the most shocking things with a grin on his face. He has the ability to make smiling threats on the lives of loved ones, the inability to picture consequences. One moment he is gentle and compassionate: *Why is your face sad, Mommy?* And other times, he has no qualms about inflicting pain, and no imagination for others' feelings at all. He draws in ink on the walls, homemade symbols that he says stand for *It's okay to kill people if you have to.* It is the hardest thing in the world to believe in his innocence.

Still new to parenthood, we are baffled and troubled. *What are we raising? Why can't we fix this?* For the first time, perhaps because I am not a woman fighting for myself, but a mother fighting for my child, need breaks me. I start talking. Perhaps because my husband is with me. Perhaps because mothering this particular child shows me myself, my need of things I don't have. Perhaps because I am fighting real despair. I am making too many mistakes, and I am not a good enough person to hold my life together, and I do not deserve grace. (No one deserves grace. That is what makes it grace.)

We ask people we love, family members, church people. *What is going on? What do we do?*

I don't know, they say. *We never had a child like that.*

We launch into a path we have not chosen, and never expected to walk: with a child we cannot understand or change. We read books, check potential diagnoses, but for every three symptoms that fit, there are two that don't, and another most troubling not taken into account at all.

I can ask for answers, but I still can't ask for help. I lie in bed every night longing for a break. If only I could ask someone to keep him for one morning a week—but I know I will not. Then my boy will break their things and ruin their pretties. I am not in the habit of seeking help, and this darkness is so overwhelming to me it feels impossible to ask anyone else to shoulder it, even for a few hours. (Do you hear the double-crossing lie? It's so dark I can't ask anyone else to help. This burden is too heavy for more than one person to carry.)

Our path to healing, for him and for us, will take years. In the months to come, we will try everything we know. We will try supplements, diet changes, a couple of Christian counselors, a family doctor, an early intervention screening, a psychiatrist's evaluation, medication, scriptural anointing with oil, family interventions. We will spend hours in prayer. We will find a mobile therapist and a behavior specialist consultant.

None of it will cure him. I want to say none of it will help him, but that is not true, because over time he will make amazing and beautiful progress; but the keyword in that statement is *time*.

We must come to terms with him as he is, our beloved son, born of our genes, who for some reason has the bent of a child with a traumatic history. He was born without natural inhibitions, born without checkpoints and certain social cues.

He is ours and we love him and we will never give up on him. And we badly need help to raise him.

What do I need in these days? I need people not to judge me and my son by his behaviors. We are trying so hard. I need a hug. I need strangers in supermarkets and playgrounds to come alongside me when it all hits the fan. *Can I grab that for you? Could I hold his hand and walk with you across the parking lot? Can I clean up that spill?* I need friends to treasure and accept my boy even when he's abnormal and naughty. I need prayer for my son. And for me. I need wisdom. Ideas. Advice, when I ask for it. I need regular break times when I can breathe and get off red alert. I need empathy. Others may not have walked in my exact shoes, but surely somewhere in the Christian church there are parents who have been through anguish. I need them to hurt with me. I need them to tell me we'll make it.

What would life be like if I took ownership for requesting the things I need?

I hate to ask. The feeling is so widespread as to be cliché. Is it the fear of being indebted? Unable to repay? Or the fear of being denied, which leaves me feeling both broken and stupid? Or my discomfort with the audacious idea that I might actually have *needs*—not just things I kind of want, like a unicorn and a candy cane and a self-laundering wardrobe, but actual needs? Dependence is my least favorite location, a distinctly un-American posture. Why is *help* so hard to say?

There's a humility in asking, an awful vulnerability—Oliver Twist with an empty bowl in his hands. What will become of me? *Please, sir, I want some more.* Must I be, as Charles Dickens writes, *desperate with hunger, and reckless with misery* before I go to such lengths?

For a Jesus follower, need should be a familiar position. I should be more aware of my inability to run solo, not less. Who am I to think myself an island of self-sustaining prosperity? I am part of a body, unable to make it on my own.

Until I am able to identify what I need, the solutions remain locked in a no man's land, inaccessible to all. Far from dumping compulsory burdens on others, stating my requests frees both them and me. For their part, they don't have to guess and hand-wring. They can see the appeal clearly and say yes or no. For myself, I don't have to outsource my wants into the hands of philistines who can't see into my brain. Who knew? I may catch the occasional ladle about the ears as punishment, but part of the human birthright is permission to verbalize my own requests.

How ironic to fight dependence on others by becoming supremely dependent on them, expecting them to notice and attend to me without my initiative. It's like dumping myself in a nursing home, nonverbal and immobile, and hoping the nurses do something about it. Part of being alive is taking proprietorship of my space in the world, accessing my own caregiving, requesting my provender. The baby needs someone to feed her, the adolescent feeds herself, but the mature hosts a potluck—and takes her place at the table.

More than anything else in life, more than marriage or grief or pastor's wifing or mental health struggles, motherhood is the thing that convinces me I need. I mess up, I don't know, I ache, I regret, I say the wrong things, I hurt people, I am not prepared for this.

More than anything else, motherhood is the challenge that grabs me by the throat and pushes me up against the wall and whispers in my face, *You do not have what it takes. You are going to die on this hill.*

Asking is pushing back against the choking. Whispering, *Not today. I have resources.*

2

LOOKING INSIDE

———

I shared two lists in this chapter, lists of things I needed when my first child was born, and when my toddler tornado was reaching gale force—things like sleep and permission and food on a plate and prayer and advice and a hug. Have you ever made a list of what you feel you need at the deepest level? Sometimes it is the first step to asking for it.

No, you do not want to become a greedy-grabby who is all for what you can get. Do you really believe that is an honest picture of who you are?

Trust me on this please, dear friend. Make a list just for you. And then pick the one that makes you cry, and open your mouth to a person who is close to you, and say the words.

I need . . .

3

A Whiplash across the Room

The Help of Medication

With deepest apologies to Horace. Also to my fifth-grade teacher, who expected better.

Season of clouds, of barren gray and dun
Close bosom friend of darkness. What is sun?
A thing of faerie.
Bitterest wind, and snow on snow
Relentless misery in this line too, no place to go;
I cannot approve thee.

And yet I could forgive if thou hadst made thy peace
And by the end of February'd ceased
Thy pestilence.
O winter, ah winter, canst not thou see
The month of March is not the place for thee?
Get hence.

Another thing I wish to say concerns your roads
I wouldn't wish them on rats or pigs or toads;
They are despicable.
Snowplows, all unwitting, have spirited away thy concrete
And left a Swiss cheese where solid and gaseous meet
In random acts of violence.

This is the time of year when I finally give the season a name: I call it This Horrible Winter That Never Ends. Then I feel badly, because it is rather terrible to look a thing in the eyes and label it something cruel.

This is the time of year when A Boatload of Snow gives way to Freezing Rain, which gives way to Record-Breaking Frigidity and back to A Boatload of Snow and around again.

This is the time of year when the cashier at the little Mennonite shop says to me, *Enjoying the nice weather?* with a perfectly straight face and I don't know what to say. It's fifteen degrees out there and the roads are awful, and the heavy gray clouds are pressing so on the land that I cannot tell if it is actually snowing or just suffocating us into the ground. I do not know whether she is serious or not. I don't think she has sarcasm in her. So I say, carefully (so that it could go either way), *Sure better than last weekend, with those frigid temperatures.* And she says, *It's supposed to get cold again, this weekend.*

This is the time of year when everyone who comments on the weather has this little gem to offer: *It's supposed to get cold again, this weekend.*

What do they think it has been!

But I know what they mean: below zero. I've seen the bottom side of zero more times in a month than I ever hope to in all my life again.

This is the time of year when I could eat myself into a stupor and not care a whit, so I arrange a series of careful deceptions, starting around nine o'clock at night. *Yes, soon I will go and make that decadent cup of hot chocolate, but first I will work on this [journal entry] [household project] [third chapter of Wendell Berry] and then after a while I will go get something tasty . . . Maybe I will have a bowl of chips too . . . Soon . . . But first I will just finish this up . . . .* If I manage very carefully I can, without actually saying no, trick myself into putting off food and drink until my pillow looks more appealing than anything else and I go to bed gratefully, with an empty stomach. I try to steer my hunger to the right things.

Once upon a time when I am in my upper twenties, I make an appointment to see our family doctor. What is more, I keep it. Yay for me.

I am here for two reasons: to request input on the hyperactivity issues of my preschool son, and to request health advice for the seasonal depression I am experiencing. We cannot go on as we are, and I am afraid. Afraid to be honest about the scale of both issues, how unusual my second son's behavior is and how intensely dark I am feeling. How we are swirling together blind in this snowstorm, gripped by forces we cannot see, only feel. My husband and I sit side by side, talking to our doctor first about our child.

She listens well. She is puzzled like us, but she doesn't freak out. I begin to relax.

We talk for a long time. Then she says, *Now, tell me about this other issue. How you feel in the winters.* I begin, falteringly, to talk about it, trying to put it into words.

She begins to frown.

The first question she asks is, *How bad is it in your worst times?*

Well, I say softly. *Um. In my worst times I have to make myself stop thinking about ending my own life.* I have never said that aloud before.

She barely gives me time to catch my breath. She flings a second question across the room, and it catches me like a whiplash. *How would you do it?*

I stagger to a full stop, because that is the one question she is not supposed to ask. I know exactly how I would do it.

See now, I'm going to hit pause right there. We have come to the place where we must consider whether pastors' wives who believe in the healing presence of Jesus have any justification for being suicidal. But, in fact, it is exactly this question that keeps me from honesty—what I should be, and what I am.

For years, I nosedive briefly after my babies' births and badly every wintertime. Why? Shouldn't the sweet provision of Christ be adequate? Shouldn't it be enough to be his? Shouldn't a holy life in his honor result in feelings of peacefulness and well-being?

A happy-go-lucky child can grow to become a woman who always has a smile, a decoration to distract from the places inside her that hurt. A lacy pinafore over the sackcloth.

A daughter of God, raised to see meaning in life's circumstances, can sit on her porch steps of an evening facing into the darkness, and see only the yellow eyes of the stars coming to get her, and behind them, nothing. She can cry, *Where are you?* and find that sometimes, no one answers.

I thought Jesus-Only was a great philosophy. Perhaps it is, for those who find themselves stripped of all earthly comforts, who are making their way the final yards to a hangman's noose for their faith. It's a good mantra to get you through lean times. But for the ongoing life of faith, it's a terrible way to walk. It's a presumptive spirituality that lunges off the pinnacles of temples, crying out for the angels to catch it. The human being needs things that are not automatically provided by belonging to Christ.

If he is all we need, let us sit naked on our rooftops and fail to feed ourselves, and see how we thrive then. Will he make us strong? Why pour a glass of water if he is living water? Why cook when he is the bread of life?

Why reach for friendship if he satisfies our souls? Why confess failure to our brothers if he is the one who forgives our sins? Why endure strong treatment for cancer if he can heal? Why ask for help when he is all-sufficient? Why receive therapy for autism? Why use crutches for a broken leg or a bandage for a bleeding finger? Why be accountable to anyone for our bad habits if the Holy Spirit can empower us to change? In foolish faith, we perch ourselves into place and wait buoyantly for the mercies that can hold us suspended in midair, ignoring the gentle, earthy rain of his generous abundance. His provision falls from heaven all around us, drawn by the gravity of our need. How can we admit that we require daily bread, but fail to admit that we require daily-everything-else?

Who can list the needs of a human body and soul?

Born and raised on the northern edge of Minnesota, I am the last person in the world who should be afraid of winter. But winter as I know it is blue-eyed, of sunshine and sparkle. When I become an adult and relocate to the southern border of a Great Lake, I find out that gray passes for a predominant color in these parts. Winters are murderous. Snow falls daily from constant and oppressive cloud cover.

Newly wed and in love, I thank Jesus for the good life he's given me. But I am lonely. My house requires little care. My husband leaves for work each day, taking our only vehicle with him. Stranded in an unfamiliar community with a total of zero family members (I counted carefully), zero close friends (likewise), and precious few people I know at all, I pace my living room and watch the snow fall. I develop what I call cabin fever that first winter, a restless emptiness and a desperate yearning for the sight of green leaves.

Spring comes, and with it the robins and the hothouse scent of the warm soil. I awake from months of silence. In April, I can remember that life is good. And life moves on.

But I cannot get off the roller coaster, and the months-long lows grow worse. There is always something to blame the emotions on—I am either pregnant (hence emotional) or post-partum (hence fragile and fatigued) or facing difficult circumstances (hence all over the map). Each fall I ride a frightening slide into tearful frustration and futility.

One January evening, about six years into marriage, I sit writing in my journal and get a strong sense of déjà vu. Suddenly I know I've written these words before. I page back and find I scrawled nearly identical entries twelve months before. This year, nothing is wrong in my external life. We are all healthy, my kiddos are growing fine, we have no major stresses, I am not hormonal. But my internal life is in shambles. I am writing despair just like last year, and the year before.

For the first time, I ask myself if I could be experiencing seasonal depression. For the first time, I take a long look at what January and February feel like.

I am buried alive in every disastrous emotion. Fear. Anger. Hatred. Despair. The world is stripped of meaning and beauty. Each winter I pray to die. I cry. I sleep. I experience physical symptoms I cannot explain or change. I am shaky and weak. My hands have trouble gripping, and I drop a lot of knives by mistake. When I am at home in the evenings, I sit and do nothing. I am swimming underwater and the pressure is crushing.

But I keep juggling life. I force myself to perform all the usual motions and attend all the usual events, though getting out of the house to be with people is like pushing through snow that's piled up to my chest. I am terribly shy and enormously afraid. I worry I will not be able to make conversation and look okay. I fear I am wearing my exhaustion like a garment, that people will take one glance at me and say, *Oh my word, honey. What is wrong?*

We start researching.

My baby blues are mild postpartum depression. The fancy title for my wintertime blues is seasonal affective disorder, or SAD, an elaborate way of saying I have trouble handling January. Also November, December, and February. Oh, and March. March is the worst. My body needs more sunlight than I am getting, and my mind cannot make it better.

Once we discover that my symptoms are seasonally affected, we take steps to cope. I buy a natural-spectrum lamp that mimics the sun's light, start swallowing vitamin D supplements, and coax myself outdoors whenever possible to soak up some fresh air and light. These are effective aids. They strengthen me through my third pregnancy and provide a whole winter of equilibrium.

I fight this bent in myself. I want to outlast the season with charisma, energy, and hope. Each year I have nice chunks of all three given to me, but I feel the diminishing, the exhausting, like salt blocks set out in the fall, licked by too many deer and raindrops. I need the sun. I need friendship. I need protein and estrogen. I need healing. I am not regaining enough ground in between.

Then comes the winter eight years into marriage. The big one.

I try hard to keep my life upbeat and busy. Maybe too busy. I mean to use my natural-spectrum lamp, I really do. But I don't know if it will actually help, and I don't start sitting with it until I crash off the end of a pitch-dark weekend. My body is postpartum again, with my dream-come-true daughter only four months old. I am homeschooling my firstborn in kindergarten.

My second son reaches new heights in the mischief and madness department, and we try to come to terms with what is driving him. We want to move out of town to the country, but our home has been on the market for three-quarters of a year without a single offer. My husband has joined our church leadership team, and we are facing related stressors.

I am trapped and all alone. I am lost and inadequate. I am depleted and worthless. My friends are sick or snowbound or out of town. I am falling into darkness and there is no one to save me. The world is so ugly. Why have we covered the good earth with paint and asphalt? Power lines choke the landscape, technology creeps into our brains, vulgarity corrupts all good things.

I find I cannot make decisions, even simple ones like which cheese to buy. Here I see Colby cheese. That is good. I can buy it in a chunk. I can buy it sliced thin for sandwiches. I can buy it sliced thick for crackers. I can buy it cut into stars and hearts. I can buy it mixed with Monterey Jack. I can buy it shredded, or crumbled, or cubed. Now I am sobbing in my car in the parking lot of a grocery store. I have a dozen prepackaged choices for how I want to buy my Colby cheese, while all around the world children are stick-limbed and potbellied from need.

At the best of times, I have moments when I wonder who is running this planet. The earth has some nasty undersides. Don't even get me started on politics, poverty, and children's rights. But ending up in tears every time I buy groceries, and not even a glimmer of finding this funny? Really?

Death looks so easy, the long, relaxing sleep. I think about it a lot. I imagine it in any form and feel no fear at all. *What if I were diagnosed with lymphoma? What if someone held a gun to my head? What if I were in a car accident? A burning building? I am trapped against my will to stay. Jesus doesn't give me a choice. I want to be with him but I guess I have to stay. Why did he make it so long? It is hard to be honest with my husband and hard not to be. Honey, don't be frightened. Couldn't you please let me go?*

I think about ways I could leave this life, even though I know it is forbidden. *This way would hurt a lot and that one would leave a mess for someone to clean up. But this one. Hmm. This one. I won't do it, but it is nice to know how to do it, in case—but I won't do it. But it is nice to know where I would do it and what I would need and how long it would take.*

All this time I am getting out of bed in the morning. I am eating fine. I am sleeping fine—more than fine. I am appearing at church and singing the songs.

My husband is worried about me. He says, *Why don't you invite some women into the darkness with you?* I hate when he is smart like that.

One Sunday school on a hideous gray weekend in mid-February, when the teacher opens the class for sharing time, I open my mouth and say the words. I get as far as *I am feeling a lot of darkness*—before I begin to cry so hard I cannot go on. Very profound words, oh yes, very well thought through, darling. But at last I have said them.

My church ladies get emotional with me. They gather around and pray for me. And they offer me things. This is a slight hazard of admitting need: people offer you things.

One lady orders me a huge boxful of unsolicited vitamins. I eat most of them. Not all at once, don't worry, that isn't my escape of choice. One gives me a Bible verse to cling to. It slips right over my head. One suggests I see a doctor.

I am affronted. See a doctor? *You know, honey,* my husband says, with his usual underhanded and devious wisdom, *that might not be a bad idea.*

I am always an obedient wife and I schedule an appointment with my family doctor.

I am going to get some health advice—a simple appointment, just that. What if she asks me if I've ever considered suicide? What if she asks me if I have a plan? No, that's ridiculous. I am listening to fears. I will go see her like a rational adult, and I will get some health advice. She will probably tell me to eat more broccoli and oranges.

By this I am trying to cover up the fact that I am terrified. It is the only way I can make myself go through with it.

You already know what she asks me. *How bad is it in your worst times?*

In my worst times I have to make myself stop thinking about ending my own life.

How would you do it?

I stammer through a minimal answer, and the most awkward doctor visit of my life. I speak with irritation laced in my voice. I push back hard. I grow red-faced and resentful. But I answer her question. I don't know what else to do, and I was raised not to lie. Then I assure her repeatedly that I am not going to carry it out.

She is a very blunt doctor. She asks if I have thought of what I will do with my children. Will I leave them provided for, or what? She asks if I've ever gone out and bought supplies. *No!* I reply firmly. *I'm not going to do it.* Besides, we already have the supplies. In the right side of the second drawer beside the kitchen sink.

I walk out of her office with a prescription for antidepressant medication. She tells my husband to keep a close eye on me.

The rest of that day, I am so angry I can hardly think straight. Angry that the doctor believes me to require medicating. Angry that she takes me seriously when I want her to laugh it off. *Well, who doesn't come up with a little exit plan now and then?* And angry beyond telling that she forces me to say what I don't want to say, goads me into betraying my secret. I am not going to do it, but now I can't. There is no doubt in my mind. Once I have told my plan, I can no longer go out by that route, and I am furious. Which means I must have been holding it closer than I thought I was.

Six weeks to feel the full effect of the medication, with the first days foggy. After just one week, I am sobered when I go back to the office for a checkup. Sobered, and beginning to feel the first twinges of fear. I realize that at some point I have spent a lot of time thinking about this plan. In what dark worlds have I been living?

In my mind, medication for mental health is anathema, the kind of thing that losers take.

Keep your shirt on; I take it. (Ecco. I am a loser.)

The question is, how will I heal?

What will you give me, to cure me? What would you prescribe? Will it be a box of vitamins, or a verse from Psalms? A chapter from history? Your best faith lessons from Scripture? Godly example?

Or a little tube of pills from the doctor's office? It is the right dosage, and will work extremely well for me in the long run.

What do I need?

Sunlight would be good, if you could bottle it for me. The only substitutes I know are artificial. Perhaps a southern clime, if you can send it north. A break from childbearing might help, though none of our three children to date were pre-planned, only pre-anticipated and pre-welcomed and pre-loved. Biblical truth will help me someday, when I finally realize I believe a lot of things that are false about our world and the intentions of Christ. But at this time, wisely worded ideas don't even leave a footprint between one of my ears and the other. I am too tired to think my way out.

My illness is one of the mind. I have not given up on Jesus, but I have given up on the earth. I cannot see how he is healing it. I am blinded in the night. It is a bitter pill to swallow, but I need little bottles of medicine from the doctor's office, a two-year nudge toward equilibrium and calm, so that I can recover my ability to feel what I feel, instead of what my brain thinks it feels. To think real thoughts, and not the false, entangling, debilitating, frenetically cycling ones. To know the truth, which will set me free.

Medication will not heal me. But for a time it will place-hold for my brain so I can breathe, so my mind can catch hold of this earth and put its roots down deep again instead of pulling away to the world to come. Life is here, where my body and brain are struggling. I need to find my place and bloom.

Medication will give me the courage to take the next step: connecting and learning.

Medication will solicit responses from other people, when I am brave enough to admit that I take it—not the judgment I perpetually expect, but instead empathy and confession. *I had to take something too, for a while.*

Medication will strip away a few layers of my frilly pretenses, because I can no longer think through subterfuge, and make me a more honest woman. A more humble woman.

Medication will be one segment of a life overhaul, one emergency response implemented alongside many others. What does my body need to be healthy? What does my mind need to be at peace?

Being a Jesus follower does not free me from needing. It does not guarantee me a happy life, or release me from the threat of loss and mental illness and broken places. Am I saying he cannot heal? I am not. His mercy can hold me suspended in midair. But counting on him to make special allowances for me because I am a special human is not the way to walk with him. I am a normal human. I need the things normal humans need.

Daniel Defoe, in *Robinson Crusoe*, says it best. *How frequently, in the course of our lives, the evil which in itself we seek most to shun, and which, when we are fallen into, is the most dreadful to us, is oftentimes the very means or door of our deliverance, by which alone we can be raised again from the affliction we are fallen into.*

For me, the evil is not depression, or even medication. The evil is cracking. The evil is calling for help. The evil is letting people in, admitting I don't have what it takes. And that evil is about to become one of Jesus' most effective tools in saving me.

3

LOOKING INSIDE

—————

LIGHT FOR SURVIVING DEPRESSION

It feels wrong to raise so many issues without giving more practical ideas for combating depression. My goal as we sit together is not to instruct you, but to share with you some of the strategies I have found helpful in fighting my darkness. If you identify with my story, which ones do you feel would make you a stronger, healthier person?

Before we begin, let me note that this isn't a substitute for medical advice or counseling. If you are thinking about hurting yourself or others, please seek help. In the United States, you can contact the National Suicide Prevention Lifeline (1-800-273-8255). Other countries have similar resources. You are not alone.

1. *Whatever your neurosis is, accept it as a stiff mercy.*
   Every human is given limitations. One of mine is depression. It is a steep grace to me, a nudge toward the help I need from Jesus and his people. I do better when I give myself permission to feel what I feel—to move forward with this troublesome travel companion instead of pretending it's not there.

2. *Eat right.*

   More fresh produce, good protein, and healthy fats. Fewer carbs and less sugar. Our bodies need the best fuel they can get just now. Try a different salad every day for lunch, topped with great meat or other proteins and bright veggies.

3. *Exercise if you can.*

   Walk for a few minutes, bundled against the cold as needed. If all you can do is step onto your porch and breathe and lift your arms to the sky, do that.

4. *Get good sleep.*

   This can be a tricky one for women in many stages. Do what you need to do: a white noise machine, a calming tea, a medically approved sleep aid, journaling before bedtime to clear your mind, asking your spouse to take his turn on night duty with the kids, sneaking a short nap when you can. Satisfying rest makes a world of difference.

5. *Explore sorrow in safe ways.*

   Though it may seem counterintuitive, I find sad songs and dark books to be my friends in times of depression. Instead of deepening the darkness, they give me a safe place to release emotion. Good poetry is healing as well.

6. *Look for truth and beauty everywhere you go.*
   Start by looking for color. Fill your house with pops of it. And while didactics will never heal depression, explore truth as you can. Christ is in this old world. He is up to something.

7. *Learn to recognize and minimize depressive triggers.*
   Holidays may be tricky, or upcoming due dates at work, or hey, grocery shopping for cheese. Say no to a few things—maybe 25 percent. Send a proxy to a few others. Bring moral support to a few more. Breathe your way through the rest. Sometimes in the winter I hand my mom a long grocery list and my debit card. She loves shopping.

8. *Maximize creative outlet.*
   What do you like? What are you good at? You might plant a pot of flower seeds, give a gift, spend time in nature, write something, or dig out your crafting supplies. Put some happiness into each week with a few tactile habits.

9. *Be with people in the ways you can.*
   Especially little people. They lift the heart. Carve out time for friendships too, even when you can't think clearly or make everything okay.

10. *Talk regularly with a trusted friend or mentor.*
   Depression should be treated as both physical and emotional, not as one or the other. We will discuss this more in our next chapter.

11. *Sit with Jesus.*
    If you can, pour out your heart to him. If you can't find words, be still with him. Take time for awareness of his presence. Fix your eyes on him as much as you are able, and know that his attention is on you too.

12. *Talk with a doctor. Consider trying medicine.*
    I list this last because I don't necessarily think it's the place to start. (If you're feeling suicidal like I was, dear one, it probably is. Can you receive that?) We can try many other things first, but let's not leave this one too long. I'll be honest with you: it helps.

Which two or three suggestions feel most doable, and why?

Which feel most daunting, and why?

4

Encounter

The Beauty of a Long-Term Mentor

In a recent national study of thousands of Christian women between the ages of twenty and sixty, 98.4 percent of them indicated a preference for losing a limb over saying the words *I can't do this. Would you please help me?*

From a linguistic standpoint, the statement does not appear to be unusually problematic. But in fact, the opposite is true. Psychiatrist Dr. Guesswho believes it to be a unique combination of phonetic sounds that creates the difficulty. His clinical study "Help Wanted" found participants able to get as far as *I can*—before going all to pieces and walking out of the examination room.

Other symptoms of distress during this exercise included racing heart, rapid breathing, and weakness in the joints. Some patients looked around the room for alternate exits. One wrapped herself in the paper sheet covering the examination table and swore like a sailor.

And she was Anabaptist, so you know it had to be bad.

O ver the back of a church pew it has happened to me. And in front of a crowd. And in a quiet room. And through my email inbox. And in small groups of friends.

It has happened to me: that moment when a woman with seniority looks into my face and sees I am looking for something I don't have, and reaches into her heart and pulls out experience that can help me.

It is one of the most rewarding connections, one of the safest places I know.

My body is resting and my mind is still, thanks to medicine. I am ready to take the next step.

One of the things I now know to be true about myself is that I've spent most of my life looking for a mother. And not because I don't have one. But because nearly every day I am in need of one, someone more experienced to advise me, someone with loving eyes to look on me, someone with a bosom to cry my tears on. I am not sure it is possible to live this close to another woman without fear, which may be why most of us push back hard at some point on the woman who raised us, determined to breathe and be our own person. But we come back—if not to her, to a surrogate—and if we cannot, we live with a craving in our bones.

I am born to a good mom. She is present and participatory, and she really cares about me. She meets my needs, provides sustenance, stability, and structure. For many years as I grow up, she and my father are my safe place, my only adult confidants. They know best what to say when I am struggling. Commitment and security make it easier to be honest. The only dilemma, which emerges somewhere in the teen years, is where to go when I am struggling with *them*. So I pick one parent to talk to about the other, but of course they share the whole caboodle in the secret Parental Communication Lab, and then I am hanging in between the two of them, and backing down.

The camp next door to Jesus-Only is Jesus-and-Family, nearly as selfish as God-and-Country. In this camp, the people Out There will not understand you, and they might even backstab you and tear you down. (So may we, but it's all in the clan. And we'll patch it up over Thanksgiving turkey.) You will probably be disappointed, and certainly exposed, if you seek anything from Others, because here we know each other and we have what it takes. Only we can look at our dirty laundry. Come to us with all your needs; we'll deal with them in-house. As long as we are a self-sustaining pod, we can maintain the illusion that we don't need anything at all. There are the people who need, and there are the people who meet others' needs, and God forbid you find yourself living on the wrong side of the tracks.

Family caring for family is a beautiful thing. Close relationship with my kin is a coveted gift. The problem is that I feel guilty self-disclosing to anyone but them, as though I am betraying family loyalty. Shattering the family heirloom:

the ability to perform no matter what. Becoming—horror of horrors—a needy person.

I have a mother but I need another. Someone who is always there, who loves me and commits herself to me for years and watches my growth with tender eyes, but with the added feature of a little perspective. Someone who won't panic if I am thinking of killing myself, but will listen and love and suffer with me, and then trust me to go home and be an adult and figure it out. Someone unlike me, so she can help me grow stronger in my areas of weakness. Someone who can take a step back and see what I am without being blinded by what I am to her.

When I talk to my family members, they are on my team, bent or broken in the same places as me. Relying solely on family is still hoeing my own row.

I want a dozen mothers. Twenty. Forty. I want one always there at the moment I fall and skin my knee, many who hold pieces of my heart, countless more who speak their words of life over me. But especially, I need one. One spiritual mother who knows the worst of all the junk, who is older and wiser, who prays for me and checks in from time to time.

Someone to carry me under her heart while I develop.

A long-term mentor falls, by the mercy of Jesus, into my lap. (But not literally.)

Just before my illusion of competence shatters in the doctor's office, that ruinous February in my eighth year of marriage, I stand in a church chatting after evening service with friends from another congregation. I know the woman I am talking to, have known her for years. I have never shared much of myself with her; I consider her my parents' friend. What I don't know is that she is a woman whom God is calling to care for other women. And that she knows far more of me than I think she does. She has run into my family's faults and sins many times before.

She looks in my eyes this night and says, *How have you been doing?*

Surprisingly, I give her a little glimpse. *It's been kind of dark,* I say.

She asks a few good questions.

I fumble for words, nervous, grateful, trying to be honest.

She puts out a little feeler. She says, *If you ever want to talk, I am here.*

I say, *I'd like that.*

Many women say that—*I am here if you ever need anything.* On the upside, there is no pressure or obligation and I can walk away without committing anything. This is nice. On the downside, there is no pressure or obligation and I can walk away without committing anything. I might have every good intention to take up a friend on her offer, but the next day I think, *Is it too soon?* And several days later, *Did she mean it, or was she just being nice?* And a week after that, *I really should reach out.* And several months down the road, *She probably forgot all about it, and I'm embarrassed to say anything now.*

This time, there is this difference. She watches me to see whether I want it or not, watches for cues about whether I am seeking, and I am, and she can tell. She says, *I'd be open to that. Let's meet, then.* Within days, she drops an email in my inbox asking when a good time would be.

At that meeting, when she has seen further in, she says, *I wonder if it would be helpful to meet once a month for a while. Would you like that?*

And I say, *I'd like that.*

A few of us stubborn and independent people require more mercy than we're willing to ask for.

One of the reasons medication helps me is that in my time of darkest struggle I am too weak to think through my pain, too overwhelmed to make the lifestyle changes that might help, too muddled to recognize my own cognitive tracks. I am unwell, and I need to rest in a safe place until my mind and body are recovered enough to go on.

But medicine, as I told you, cannot heal everything. Medicine does not address who I am, it only buys me space from my demons. Sometimes that space is absolutely essential. But it's only part of the cure.

If I am going to heal in a lasting way, if I am going to become a person who can embrace the world without wincing away, I am going to need restoration at the level of my faith and hope and personhood. How? Cognitive truth is abstract and disembodied. I find no place to catch hold of it. What does it matter? It is just words, a puff of hot air. When I crack because my world is imploding around me and I cannot be strong anymore, the last thing I need is someone offering helpful instruction. *The Bible has this to say about that. You see, it's not the way you think. What you need to understand is this.*

Words can change me, clean me, heal me—and they can zip right over my head. They can hurt me, betray me, distract me—and they can lead me home. I must find a significant series of them to allow a mentor into my darkness. She cannot magically look into my mind without them. And she must find some in order to influence me. Words. But I cannot access truth through them myself. I cannot pull them off a page, even the most holy of pages; they slip from my reach; I cannot tie them to solutions. The words of truth I need nestle in relational connection, a cradle of contact and reality. Something tangible to grasp the body so the spirit stays to listen.

Jesus' ministry was an enormously touching one, when you think about it. There was a shocking quantity of skin and hands and sweat and mud and spittle. And he wrote fairly big and bold in the margins—touching the untouchables, breaking the taboos. Inviting children to sit on the rabbi's lap. Welcoming the caress of a woman's hair on his feet. Reaching to place his hand on a dead body, ceremonially unclean. Letting strangers cry all over him. Touching the wounds of the quarantine ill. Kneeling to wash dirty toes.

He fed people a lot. Ate with them. Fished with them. Walked the roads alongside his friends.

In his whole life on earth, you never see Christ sitting pretty onstage, handing out sterile gold nuggets of inspiration. You see him dusty, exhausted, wakeful, hungry, jostled, bleeding, shouting, silent: but never, ever disembodied or detached. Always human, always someone you could catch hold of and connect to. A divine encounter through living flesh.

When the thousands of grasping hands became too much and there was nothing left to give, he stepped back for a night and rested in his Father under the stars. Then he walked back across the sea and started all over again.

I have longed for the hand of Christ on my head. What would his arms feel like around me when I am breaking? There is only one way to experience this knowledge in my body—it is to allow myself to break in an encounter with a human being who carries his Holy Spirit within her. What happens when I meet another person without my protective gear? Divine encounter through living flesh.

We may treat pain as spirit (offer truth) or emotion (share a tissue) or mind (ask good questions) or body (bake a casserole), but each piece cut off from the others is just a superficial patch-up job when it is the soul, the personhood, the being, that is shattered.

I don't need to *hear* what is true, I need to experience it. The way I experience it is in skin, when someone sits with me, gives me a hug, holds both my hands while she prays. I need my soul and body tied back together. I need a place to crack while being held securely intact, a baby wailing from the safest place on earth: her mother's love. I cannot always be the mommy, handing the nurture around. Sometimes I must be the child, the human, the small creature in need of mercy. Sometimes I am fresh out.

There is so much talk about God as the Father, coming to him as Abba. I want to know God as my Mother. The One who knows how to make it better. Life giver, food bringer, tender nurturer. Ever vigilant, always close. A fistful of his tunic clutched in my hand.

In this enlightened age of cutesy self-presentation and self-nurture, I forget that truth and healing are supposed to be interpersonal, and are nearly always messy. We are meant to be changed in the context of presence. Relational connection is transformative, and at its best is designed to draw in all of what we are: not just our minds and our feelings, but our spaces and our bodies. Not our smiling public image, but our private joys, our fears, our needs.

When I first experience connection with a mentor at this level, it doesn't feel like a good thing, an emergence. It feels like the breaking of all I've tried so hard to hold together. I hate how it feels. My unbeautiful story laid out in the open. A messy history. Unguarded tears when I don't expect them. When I expose the cracks in my heart, I face enormous fear of being rejected, being too much, breaking crucial things.

It takes a lot of stripping to let someone this close. Not only my armor, but my independence, my adulthood, my self-possession. My normal skin. I find it the emotional equivalent of appearing at a coffee shop in my underwear, becoming ready to do life some other way than all by myself. It's terrifying. What will she think? I want to pull the covers back over me, apologize for my faults, describe and defend and explain too much, dodge away when things turn sensitive. Then I see that the look in her eyes is not criticism. It is knowledge and love.

> *I sit on my porch steps and feel invisible,* I say. *I don't know if Jesus is even watching.*
> She says, *His eyes are on you forever.*
> And I can see this truth in hers.

> *I cannot mother this child,* I say.
> *He chose you and trusted you with him,* she says. *You will find a way.*
> And she gives me a hug.

> *The world would be better off without me. I'm sure. I am ruining too much,* I say.
> She says, *He made you for a reason.*
> *I love to talk with you.*

It hurts, I say.

She says, *You can cry. It's okay.*

And she puts her hands on my head and prays.

Neither my own mind nor medicine nor time nor dogmas can identify the lies and gently swap them out for the truth. But relationship? Maybe relationship can.

It is possible that if I lose my armor in front of another woman, she might care for me.

Sometimes our family watches nature documentaries and animal kingdom shows. A frequent scenario recurs: a predator pack moving in on the herd. The wolves start sneakily, shadows among the trees. They groom the edges of the herd, checking, checking. What are they looking for? The loners. The prey too small or ill or foolish to stay with the community. When they spot one, it is a simple matter of inciting just enough panic in the intended victim to make it perform its own intuitive self-destruction: veering off from its companions on a wild tangent, desperate to hide.

You can never let anyone know that part of you. No one will understand. They will hate you. Everyone else is doing fine. What an embarrassment you are.

My little girl fidgets in her chair, her horrified eyes glued to the screen as the wolves chase the vulnerable one. We turn down the nerve-shattering soundtrack. We bite our nails and root for the bunny, or whatever it is this time: the newborn mountain goat, the dehydrated antelope, the injured seal. The wolves move in, bolder now, swift, intent.

It all comes down to this crux. Will the intended victim have the strength to rejoin the pack?

Or will its blood spatter the snow?

I often feel that I owe it to God to be a success story.

I tell you the truth. The greatest heartbreak of Christian womanhood in my time is isolation, when we are so busy keeping our smooth images intact that we don't even notice we are imprisoned behind them. We may be lonely and inadequate and terrified and empty. But ooh we are looking good.

Solitude is what kills us.

Am I so afraid of the real Christians all around me who are doing it properly instead of desperately winging it? Am I the only one? Will it ruin everything if I admit my sin? That the pastor's wife can't manage her children or behaved like a terrible mom today or wants to die sometimes on dark nights?

Perhaps there are less painful ways to connect. But for me, the breaking of my self-sufficiency is where Christ meets me in his redeemed community. Neediness connects me to other people, who are fighting their own private battles. Failure to hold life together opens me to bounteous, unforgettable resources that I can never access when I am going all DIY.

And I notice I feel better. Clean. Open. Renewed.

Who are you and what do you do?

I am a mother.

Why not a friend or cake baker or carpet vacuumer or wife?

Mothering is engrossing, no doubt about that. But so is breathing, and friendship. I wonder why I pick this piece with which to self-identify most often. Can it be I am most comfortable with myself as a need meeter, food maker, nurturer? If I say *I am a daughter*, for example, the label carries with it all kinds of loving and smothering, me on the receiving end of the action instead of the action provider. Why do we all want to baby our kids, but few of us allow our mothers to get too close?

I don't need you to mother me, I am a mother now myself. I am a big girl. I can meet my own needs. I can deal with my own messes.

Here is my question. How can we give what we are not receiving? Not only *what we have not received*, as though once and done will fix it, but *what we are not in ongoing ways receiving?*

How can I be an adequate mother until I have learned to be a daughter? To nestle into the security of being fully loved, fully accepted, with my needs met and my provision ready? No one of sense wants to be a sponging recipient of all the goods, but honestly, I can't take care of me just because no one else is doing it. Mothering is meant to be generational, a passing of care from oldest to older to old to young to younger to youngest. Rows and rows of women cared for in turn by those who have been down this path already and aren't afraid of what they see, who nurture and give and soothe without fear. Without it, we self-exhaust from the inside out.

When you ride an airplane, the flight attendant tells you to fasten your own mask first. So selfish, no? If you have only thirty seconds, wouldn't you rather use it to save another's life? But we have more than thirty seconds. We have a whole life. With a little oxygen, I become able to save many lives. I can never be so needed that I don't have time to receive. That's an oxymoron and a juxtaposition and a disaster. The more I am needed, the more I must make sure I am breathing. Dead people can't save anybody.

I realize I will need someone to help me. I need someone with whom I don't have to try harder, live stronger, pull it together. I need to pour out my heart without a filter and know that she'll sort it.

When I encounter the motherlove of God in a human (and in more than one human), I will lay my head against it and breathe and let go. The need to be grownup and together. The fear of what she might think. The consequences of life's choices. I receive the arms around me, the wholehearted kiss on my cheek, the inexpressible comfort of believing it's going to be okay because she says so. I become older and younger, rocked, treasured, held.

I encounter her, this mother who is cheering me toward Christ. I encounter the Father, the heart of love that never lets go and never depletes. I encounter myself, my smallness and sorrow, my need, my hope of healing, my hunger. I meet these three at the intersection and call it mentoring. Receiving grace.

He knows I am going to make it because he made me, he is abundantly able, and he sees all things.

She knows I am going to make it because she has seen me do it before. Because she has tools that will help me. And because she's not going to quit until I do. She is *with*: the most sacred word known to humans.

I know I am going to make it because they know I will.

I will sit on her couch every month, over and over. In her office chair. For months that add up to years, she will carry me in her heart as I grow. She will share me with the Father, cheer for each milestone, remind me how far I've come, let me go back and be small again and safe. I will uncover things she has never dealt with, but the Holy Spirit will enable and equip her. She will learn from her own mother, and she will teach me. She will love.

What is your greatest desire?
To be fully seen, and fully loved.
This is divine encounter in the flesh.

4

LOOKING INSIDE

THOUGHTS ON FINDING A MENTOR

Hello again. Do you have someone who nurtures you in regular and ongoing ways? If not, here are some suggestions for finding a friend who can do it.

1. *Recognize your need.*
   Must the world be divided into the people who offer help and the people who seek it? What do you wish you could share with someone about? How would you like to grow? What might you receive?

2. *Let go of your desire to find The Perfect One.*
   You won't find a woman who's been through all the same experiences you have, or who understands you completely and cares for you perfectly. If you start analyzing perks of different personalities, subliminal

nudging of the Lord, mutual history, and whether or not she makes good coffee, you can muddle in indecision forever.

When I think of a mentor, I think (a) same gender, (b) older than me, and (c) serious about her walk with the Lord. Make a short list of three women in your community who fit those criteria, and with whom you'd be willing to talk honestly.

Then pick one and . . .

3. *Ask.*

This is the hardest part.

Be clear in what you are asking. Are you seeking skills coaching, a listening ear, advice for change, or prayer support? How often? Many women are honored to be asked to walk with a younger woman, especially if they know what you're hoping for. Others will not feel up to the challenge, and that is okay. Go to the next person on your list. You will not know if the door is open until you try the handle.

4. *Receive her input.*

   Your mentor may think differently than you expected. She may push you toward paths that feel uncomfortable. No one should be god in your life but God, yet having asked for input, you would be foolish to brush it aside lightly. Consider her words. Talk to a friend and the Lord about them. And hang in there while you get accustomed to one another. There will be inevitable bumps, where something strikes you wrong or you have trouble communicating clearly with each other. If the relationship doesn't gel, don't force it. But your goal is connection that lasts. Do not cycle through counselors in search of one who will say the right things.

5. *Don't make it all about you. Or her.*

   If you don't care about her experiences, and care only about sharing your own, you're in trouble. If she becomes the only one who can listen well, advise right, or walk with you, you're in even bigger trouble. Keep sharing your friendship and trust with a wide range of women. It's never wise to hinge your honesty, stability, or support on one person.

6. *Say thank you.*

   Find ways to bless her back. She is giving of herself, and her generosity is worth acknowledging. You in turn have gifts that will mean a lot to her. Use them well.

How do you feel about the idea of a spiritual mother?

What are your wishes and hopes for this kind of relationship?

What will be the most difficult part?

5

Tyranny of the Urgent

The Power of Procrastination

———

It is impossible not to finish something
If you keep plugging away at it.
This is what I tell myself
When my projects look overwhelming.

On the other hand,
I suppose it is impossible
To finish something
If you keep plugging away at it.

So it would appear
That the better part of success
Is knowing when to keep plugging and
When to quit.

When I am a child, I am a scatterbrain and an airhead, leaving a trail of breeze and butterflies and missing articles behind me. I flit. I know the secrets of the universe—the new leaves, the seeds I tucked into the soil, the feel of a butterscotch kitten.

Responsibility teaches me to become organized and efficient as I grow, to always know where my gear is and where I'm going on Thursday and what the next fifteen steps should be. To measure my days by what I accomplish, by the successes I mark.

Not by the dandelions and wild roses I find.

THANKSGIVING WEEK, NINTH YEAR OF MARRIAGE

Monday. I unpack from a weekend trip, wash a bunch of laundry, bake cakes, go grocery shopping, have dinner with my husband's colleagues, and miss an evening event for my church ladies because my husband has a conflicting meeting—and one of us needs to stay with the kids. Not that I'm bitter about this.

At ten o'clock at night, my second son is running a nonstop monologue over a sheet of stickers, expecting me to interject occasional comments and replies. He cannot sleep, and we have let him out of bed, not knowing what else to do. I always put him down for a nap in the afternoon because a whole day of caring for him without a break is insanity. I am probably a bad mom because of this.

My husband is on the phone with his father, sharing plans I didn't know we had. Three weeks ago, we bought the ramshackle home of our dreams: ten acres of wild land, an elegant aging farmhouse, a creek. Now we have work to do, and the landlord of the rental we are living in has decided to put our residence on the market. In the past week, a realtor visited five times, always last minute. *I need to come by to measure rooms,* she says. *I need to stop over to take pictures. Can you do a showing at nine o'clock tomorrow morning?*

Tuesday. Ladies from church are getting together to sew. I am responsible for bringing homemade decorated cakes for a friend's birthday, but it turns out she may not be there, so I need an alternate plan. We have that house showing, which means I need to leave our spaces tidy.

My daughter is sixteen months, a precious stage, beginning to role-play Mama with her own dolly, while still needing me every few minutes for her own diaper changes and feedings.

Tonight my husband's place of work is hosting a staff dinner, and I cook and contribute a gallon of soup as requested.

Wednesday. My firstborn has a half day of school today, with a famous Thanksgiving lunch exchange—a special lunch in a creatively decorated box to swap with a friend. I need to clean my rental house and make food for this weekend. Meanwhile, I spend hours at our newly purchased house, doing the inexplicable job of pulling hundreds of nails out of the wood floors in three rooms. I can see nailheads on the insides of my eyelids.

I cannot get around to urgent things. There are library books and phone calls to return, a checkbook to balance, nails to trim and haircuts to give.

My second son pees down the furnace vent. He plays trampoline on my bed, just like yesterday and the day before and the day before, despite my consistent correction and discipline. What am I not doing? How can I fix this? I put a stop sign on the wall above the bed, so he can see the rules, and it works.

I am a good cook, but of course two of the three concoctions I bake today flop. I don't bake my turtle bars long enough and they come out mushy. My pitas do not poof. Why am I making pitas?

Thursday. We spend Thanksgiving Day with my family, feasting and enjoying ourselves. In the evening, the first of our weekend company arrives.

Friday. My in-laws descend in bulk to help with the house for the weekend. I love that they are doing this for us. We have a tiny rental, so everyone is staying in hotels and coming over during the days for meals and projects. What will we eat?

DECEMBER, NINTH YEAR OF MARRIAGE

After the weekend, two men stay and move into our rental with us: my father-in-law and brother-in-law. They spend their days employed by my husband, working on our new house. I cook soup and bake meatloaf and brew countless pots of hot coffee.

My oldest son rides the bus to and from school. One day I am working at the new house and nearly forget to return to the rental in time for his drop-off. I pull in just as the school bus does, and get goosebumps thinking of how close my six-year-old came to finding his home unexpectedly empty, his family gone without a word.

I must stay on top of these things. I must.

I watch my second son carefully. I don't know at what moment an event will set him off into aggression and hostility.

I am always stopping mid-motion. Raised voices in the living room bring me running, knowing I have mere seconds before an object is thrown or a person is pushed to the floor.

One of the awful things about being a mom is the startling things that come out of your mouth. *Yes, picking up toys is not always fun, but we must do it anyway. Please don't put your fork in my face. If you fall in the toilet doing that, I'm not fishing you out. Everything you two fight over, I am taking away—you get no toys at all until you learn how to* PLAY.

(Excuse me, could you come again on that?)

There is always work to be done, always someone to feed, always someone who needs me. Countless projects bellow at us from the new house: kitchen cabinets to refinish, junk to empty from abandoned rooms, wallpaper to strip, flooring to remove. I teach kids' club at our church, not that well. There is always work to be done.

I accidentally leave my journal open on the counter overnight, and my husband sees the open spread of my questions and fears. I awake with an edge of a headache and a touch of regret and a stockpile of shame. I am irritable with my second son all morning—he drops everything and he is freakishly irrationally unkind and he never stops talking. I shout at him. Again. And again.

Now the shame is creeping above my ears and it is drowning me.

I am yelling at him because life is yelling at me and I don't know how to make it stop.

I am such a woman. Emotional. Prone to drama. When I work on our new home, I feel my femininity, my inadequacy, the things I didn't get trained to do and the others I can't do because I am not smart enough. Or muscled enough. I cannot tell which bothers me most.

I want so much from myself.

Under my hand, our minivan mires itself down into the inches-deep mud in our new yard. In my paint-and-mud-streaked dress and stained coat, with long pants underneath for the cold, I carry gravel by the shovel load to throw under the stubborn tires. I scoop away mud. I wipe my dirty fingers on the grass, shove myself against the van in neutral, pull out some boards to use as planks. I push. I pray. I employ questionable language. And in the end, I taste failure and impotence. Woman 0, Vehicle 1.

When my husband comes, he puts the right things under the tires and has the van out in ten minutes.

That evening I attend a Christmas banquet. I am pristine in a long red dress, a white shirtfront, and a slim black sweater with a belt. Black boots. With my children swirling around me, I am a madonna and a queen. I have crafted an elegant dessert. I sip sparkling virgin punch from a goblet. I look at my name, *Shari Zook*, in elegant script on the place card, and I remember the mud.

Whatever the world needs from me, that is what I give it.

JANUARY, NINTH YEAR OF MARRIAGE

Lake-effect snow is trying to bury us. My husband returns from his day job at six in the evening, after helping a woman whose vehicle slid into the ditch. He can get other people's vehicles out too, not only his own. He must meet a buddy at the new house by six thirty. He has half an hour to be a daddy and to eat the supper I made.

My husband can do what he needs to do. I handle the fallout, and not that well.

We have boxes stacked high in our rental. Each day I pile a few more. The house is drafty, poorly made. I find my daughter's bedroom window wide open. My son opened it to scoop snow from the porch roof onto the carpet, and *forgot to close it, Mommy, sorry*. The roads are impassible and we still don't have a moving date.

When the snowplows get through, we host the church's small group at our house and I make a snack. I am always making food, and it is never filling me.

I wish I were doing something useful and beautiful. I wish I could make a difference. So much is calling our names. But when my husband and I take the three kids along so we can try to work together, they hang about getting in trouble and my daughter hugs our knees and cries. Both of my sons get into the mud and one of them puts gravel down the drainpipes.

Packing for the third move in eight months wouldn't be so bad if it weren't for the small helpers. They remove stuff from already packed boxes and they whine and need food or stories or cuddles and you have to work around all the naptimes and when you're distracted, they get a screwdriver and start removing hardware from your interior doors.

What if I am pregnant again?

I unload my dishwasher and get my kids a snack and stop working to read them a story or two and make pizza for supper and pack another box. My hair needs to be washed and the children need baths tonight and I teach Sunday school tomorrow.

The night before our move, the kitchen sink and both toilets are finally set into place. I never thought I'd say hallelujah over a toilet, but I'm saying it now. Our living room floor is still dirty bare wood and there are rooms we have hardly touched.

But at last we are home. We have the rest of our lives to settle in.

My husband works until two in the morning refinishing the open stairway before his brother comes to lay a carpet runner down it. Gorgeous wood, rich and shining.

I practice my own shining descent through the snow, my sons in front of me on the sled. We whip down our hill—our own hill!—through the weeds and woods, speeding into our yard. We laugh hysterically with the thrill of it. *Mommy, let's do it again,* they beg and of course we do, over and over, no urging needed. Our feet are cold and our legs scratched and skinned, but oh boy.

We are home.

The real downer about being raised to be so responsible is that if I am not careful—if I am too careful—I miss all the seren- dipity. Some of us who grew up on *Why put off till tomorrow what you can do today?* and *A job worth doing is worth doing right* need to learn that there truly is a tomorrow, in which we can work, and that a job done improperly still blesses the family. Doing things not that well is part of life. A good way to get through, and to grow.

Raising a difficult child teaches me that parenting is about emergency interventions. Coming alongside my husband as he renovates a house on short order and pastors a church teaches me the same. When stuff needs doing, red alert. It must be done now, and it must be done well. But then I am becoming a performance machine, at the mercy of anything that whistles at me. This is not a good way to live a sustaining life, one that includes a few dandelions.

My generation, by and large, grew up with parents who gave us a lot of tether. We look back and shake our heads at the unwatched hours in the creek, the summer afternoons playing unsupervised with cousins, the nights alone in the dark with our fears. Sometimes we needed real help we didn't get. But you have to admit we grew up pretty capable, pretty strong.

Today's parenting equates presence with participation. A good mom plays on the floor with her children and usually says yes to requests to read stories or go to the park. She talks all the time, affirmations and blessings and reassurances and life. She might sleep with her children. She keeps a hand nearby when the balance beam is being attempted, and provides helmets and elbow pads for biking. (We hardly knew what seatbelts were, and those of us who didn't die grew up learning how to brace ourselves for the railroad tracks and the potholes.)

Today we feel that parenthood equals 200 percent commitment of time and energy. Good mothering demands more than it used to, which may be partly why I yell at my kids so much more than my mother yelled at me. She had a lot more emotional freedom, more quiet hours while we were stalking black bears in the woods.

So easily, I turn my child into my perfect project, and in love and codependence I make it my job to turn him out right and prevent all bad things from happening to him. The same with my community. So easily, I make my world—life itself—my project and my child. I take it under my wing and promise to always be there for it, to fix all its issues and meet all its needs. I vow to steer this wagon right.

The world deserves a chance to right itself, to lumber slowly along in approximately the right direction. The church deserves a chance to find out what happens when I am not the first name on every sign-up sheet. Who else might take a meal to that new mom if I don't jump on in the first five minutes? My child deserves a chance to experience disappointment, failure, inadequacy, mild fear and danger, because that is how growth happens.

In a world where God, the faithful Father, is so slow to jump in and miraculously intervene (unless there is a whistle he responds to that I haven't found yet—always a possibility), why am I so sure that good parenting, good living, involves instantaneous response? Part of his genius is his patience. *I am always with you. But I do not often step in to fix and rescue what you can figure out—or learn from.*

If I don't answer the urgent request for help or funds or information, it's possible someone else will have what it takes. If I don't dash into the playroom at every whimper, it's possible (not likely, but possible) that my children will settle their own fight.

I learn best by doing. I learn that a first-time pita baking session is not a good idea in a busy week. That hosting small groups doesn't work well while I am moving homes. I learn that even if my four-year-old son is violent, he cannot usually hurt anyone too badly with a Little Golden Book. I can help him tape torn pages, give a hug to say I'm sorry, mop up his sister's spilled cereal.

I wouldn't describe myself as a helicopter parent, but maybe I am, maybe more than I think. As my children grow, their dependence on me to fix their problems frustrates me. But that is what I am teaching them all those months as I come in swinging, the magic mother with the miracle solutions and superhuman energy. How can they learn problem-solving except by problem-solving? By Mom occasionally giving them the gift of trust? They, too, learn best by doing.

I replace the soundtrack of *Why am I never there in time? Why can't I watch him better? What kind of a mother am I? What kind of a child am I raising? I am not enough!* with new songs.

This is how growth happens. No matter how perfectly I parent, my child will still be a child, messy and selfish and clumsy and precious. Self-resolution and experiment are part of healthy child development. I am not supermom, and that is okay. It is not my job to prevent life from touching them. But I am here.

Do I have to be successful to feel good about myself?

How do I decide what the day's work should be, and whether my food making and bathroom cleaning and box packing is less important than my husband's floor leveling and drywall hanging and varnish brushing? Or whether I should bundle myself and my children into the cold and spend the day on the hill? Who is to say what a woman is worth, her day's work laid out done? mostly done? not done?

Who is to say what is useful and beautiful?

Why should the thing that screams the loudest win?

The moments I treasure most from this wild winter are not the productive ones, when the kitchen cabinets are finally rehung or the sixth coat of red paint is successfully applied to a wall. I treasure the memories of walks in the cold, snuggles with my husband when he returns, a joyful hour of sledding with my son when there are boxes to unpack.

I long to find ways to tune out the things that are shouting at me in order to hear the things that are asking mutely, watching from the quiet corners of my heart, silent, peripheral. How do I do this? The most important things in life do not come with alarms and flashing red lights. Like being home for my six-year-old. No one is shrieking at me to get this done, but it is one of my best jobs.

Sometimes all it takes is pausing for a moment and looking inside and out. Looking at the state of my heart and the faces of my children. Thinking, *What is driving me here? Is it worth it?* Other times, it means blocking out chunks of time for non-events that matter to me, white spaces for relationship and rejuvenation. Other times, refusing to punish myself for declining to accomplish it all.

One potluck morning at church, when I am expected to bring one hot dish and one cold, I forget to prepare my usual offering of delectable food. I awake Sunday morning with the knowledge, but know instantly what I will take. A hot five-dollar pepperoni pizza to go (the pizzeria is five blocks from church), and a half gallon of black raspberry ice cream. I delayed! and what a peaceful Sunday morning we had! and how the church's children scarfed up my contributions! and how the painstaking creations of my sisters sparkled brighter on the buffet line!

You can take some shortcuts and no one will get hurt. You can put off some things until later.

You think I am speaking heresy? Me too. I feel so guilty even saying the words.

I am not suggesting that we should start being slothful, dropping our duties, cutting our corners. (When was the last time we were in danger of that, darling?) I am saying that all the good parts of life get squished out by the noisy parts. I can be so focused on making a gourmet breakfast for once that I don't see the face of the child who would be supremely happy with cold cereal and his mom's lap. My husband and I can power full speed ahead into myriad responsibilities and forget that we need a home base to power from, and that there are others in this world who are well able to step up and carry part of the burden.

When I delay, I give someone else a chance to mature.

And I give myself permission to be something other than supermom—an unreachable image we all carry around on our resumes or wish lists. She is tantalizing from a distance. Up close, she is flat, predictable, and utterly unenjoyable.

Managing perfectly can be yet another means of saving myself and maintaining control. Do I always have to look good? Does it always have to be me? If I am so perfect that I never let anything go, how will others grow into strength? How will I?

This superhero complex of Atlas holding the world on his shoulders is not a healthy self-image. Just saying. Call it egotism if you like, but I've always been pretty sure that if I stop doing my job, the world will fall. Each moment, I convince myself that what I am doing is of supreme urgency and importance: if I don't pull off that five-star dinner on demand, or get the kids perfectly dressed and there on time, or arrive beforehand to help set up the event, I will be personally responsible for the disintegration of everything.

In the coming years I learn to simplify and streamline. To buy the bread instead of making it from scratch when my days are full. To improvise meals and snacks, even for guests, with the contents of my pantry and freezer instead of going out to buy. To substitute. To lower a few expectations and let go of brilliant ideas, making do with very good options. To use paper plates, and to wait to clean the floor until Friday even though it's a little dirty now, and to leave the baths till evening and the grand closet sorting till spring. (Or maybe spring of next year. It depends.) To be comfortable in not being caught up with all the things at once.

I don't have time to be all I want to be, including a gentle mother, when I am spending so much time being what I don't want to be.

When I am a child, time is nothing but the slow passing of the sun through the June sky. When I am newly married, time is elastic, and I sleep in dreamily and stretch my work to fit the day until my love comes home. When I am grown, time becomes useful, and stretches to hold all I cram into it each day, enormous amounts of work and accomplishment. Later still, I gain the ability to let my time relax. To grant each day its own share, and bump a little off until tomorrow. To be five minutes late without apology, or to skip making the two-hour fancy dessert I intended to contribute in favor of chocolate chip cookies, which take ten minutes to stir up. To know that there is another time. Another day. To stop slaving for my planner and task list. To unlearn excessive obligation. To measure joy by both breezes and perfect pitas (fourth attempt), by both butterflies and clean floors.

Is that my medication talking? Or wisdom? Or laziness?

Who is to say?

But listen. I am not one of those moms who will look back and say, *Just enjoy them while they're little. I wish I'd let the cleaning and the housework go and snuggled them till they were twelve. They grow up way too fast.* I think she forgets that cleaning and housework was one of the things that helped them grow. That enjoying a relatively clean space which they helped to clean and taking charge of folding their own laundry taught them how to live well, how to catch hold of life and work hard. Responsibility is mostly good—toxic only when carried to extremes and wrapped around identity. As with all of life, balance is the essential sixth sense.

Here is what I have learned through hanging artwork on my fridge and arranging clean dishes in the drainer: Life wants to fit together. Things want to be well. There will be enough space for everything that matters, even if I do not do them in the right order or crowd them tight or arrange them just so. I discover this each time I pack a square tote for traveling. Everything nestles. The world wants to be harmonious, one of the strongest evidences for a God above. I embrace the piecemeal organic and I let it grow.

Breathe, little mama.

Go sled down a hill and whoop it up into the wind.

Start with the things that are important, and then move on to the urgent.

One spring day I sit under trees in a park, the new-blown leaves an indescribable shade of light. I lie back against the trunk, my shoulders on the moss, and I look up into a depth I cannot imagine. Rocked in the bosom of Abraham—this is what they always meant. After a time I sit up and try to journal what I feel, but immediately I lose the sweet sense of presence. I put aside my book and pen and lie down, and I come into his presence. I am alone in the arms of the Father, and nothing matters but his eyes. There is a roaring in the treetops.

5

LOOKING INSIDE

———

Make a list of all the things you do, or must do, or want to do, or are about to have done. Which are screaming at you? Which are waiting quietly? Which are essential?

URGENT | **IMPORTANT**

How can you reduce urgency and find ways to do what matters most? Inhale. Love. Trust. Succeed.

6

Sorority

*The Saving Grace of Girlfriends
(Especially When the Men in
Your Life Are Being Outrageous)*

PRELUDE
SONG OF AN AVERAGE MOTHER

————

I'll sing you a song
A song of a mother
A song of a mother who couldn't.

> Her name was Barb. For seven years she yearned for a
> child, prayed and agonized and beat on heaven's door. WHY
> CAN'T I HAVE ONE, ONE OF MY OWN? He gave her seven, and
> the second she named Shari.

I'll sing you a song
A song of a mother
A song of a mother who didn't.

She never had a child. The world became her baby, and she rocked it. She fed it warm soup and wise words while the dark closed in around her. The name she chose for herself was Teresa, but you know what they called her? Mother.

I'll sing you a song
A song of a mother
A song of a mother who wouldn't.

Her name was Klara. Come of old peasant stock, she married a twice-widowed man and faithfully tended his two children. She birthed six babies, and lost four of them painfully, to diphtheria and measles. A devoted mother, quiet and affectionate, she attended church regularly with her children, kept house, cooked meals. She would not live to see her son's career, nor the grief he carried for losing her. His name was Adolph Hitler.

I'll sing you a song
A song of a mother
A song of a mother who shouldn't.

Married to her cousin, she gave birth to a child she knew she could not keep, a child born with a death sentence. But when she saw that handsome little face, like one the stars had kissed, she simply could not let him go. At the risk of harsh legal action against herself and her son, she tried to keep him: hushed his cries, kept him hidden away in back rooms, pretended he did not exist—and when he became too big and lusty for such subterfuge, she gave him up of her own free will, and left him for another woman to raise. His name was Moses.

I'll sing you a song
A song of a mother
A song of a mother who can't.

Her name is Shari. Most days her mothering looks less like "Raising the Next Jim Elliot" and more like "Dick and Jane Gone Haywire, Sally and Spot Still Missing." When she sings around the house she hopes the neighbors are listening, but at least once a day she speaks words she hopes they miss. She worries that this is not as it should be, but in the meantime her daughter needs hugging and the laundry needs folding. Mothering makes her need Jesus a lot. She cares deeply about her children and also cares about a few things entirely unconnected and slightly incompatible with them, such as lengthy conversations, old books, and lush herb gardens.

I'll sing you a song
A song of a mother
A song of an average mother.

For all the talk about falling in love, the magic and power of it, the heartbreak of it going bad, I will tell you what is just as powerful and more transformative: sisterhood. For thousands of years, our species knew this. We women beat our clothes clean on the river rocks while talking over our lives, coparenting our children, getting wise about cyclical moons and food preparation and the foibles of the menfolk. We trusted each other. We preserved places of strict femininity, like the kitchen and the market, the secrets of the birthing room.

When humanity matured, we turned in our river rocks for a fully automated Whirlpool.

Bad trade.

On the night my boyfriend asks me to marry him, when the sand is warm under our feet and the sun is sinking over the lake, my heartbeat spikes and my answer is nontraditional. *Can we talk about it?*

I do not see his question coming, and I have been watching for a chance to talk to him about a particular worry. By now I am serious about loving him, but when I look into our future together, I foresee him being in high demand, and I worry. He is a man of many gifts. He will be shoulder-tapped often and signed up for public ministry. Our church selects pastors from the laity, and trains them in office. (In this way we do our best to ensure equality, fraternity, and lifelong humility.) I am sure he will be called to pastoring.

In fact, I am so certain of it that I speak to him about it that night, as we sit on the beach under the sunset and he waits for my final answer. *I don't know what a wife and kids will do to your life and ministry,* I say. *We might hold you back, need stuff, demand too much. I want you to be able to pursue what you are made for, get as good as you possibly can be.* I want to be sure that I am what he needs, and I am not sure.

He tells me the right things. That life together is what he wants. That he believes marriage will make him more a man of God with things to offer the world, not less.

There is no doubt in my mind that he is all I need. I am willing to leave all things for him: my father and mother and siblings, my virginity, my independence, the community in which I've lived for ten years. We will probably be the ultimate couple, the two who have no separateness between them. I am giddy with the knowledge that I am the most important person in his world. I am in love. And I say, *Yes*.

Fast-forward three years, and the man I love is selected to help lead a church plant our congregation is starting nearby. This sobers but does not surprise me. Beneath my trepidation is the surety that we are on the path laid for us before the ages, that my husband has what it takes to be a pastor, and that we can now be what we were meant to be, together. We are confident and frightened and immature and blazing for Jesus.

Fast-forward another six years, and we have been burned a few times and have learned a few things about need. We are settling into our brand-new ancient house, with our work cut out for us for years, when my husband thinks it would be a great time to add something new.

That fall, he stops by a local fire station, half a mile from our new house, and asks for an application as a volunteer firefighter.

WHAT! I say.

I don't think this is a good time, I say.

Where did this come from?

I didn't know you wanted to be a firefighter.

They have training every Tuesday night?

Really?

What about all the other irons we have in the fire? I say.

All the time it will take to renovate our house?

And your pastoring responsibilities?

And your KIDS? Whom I will be caring for?

Have you thought about how much time this might take? I say.

For no compensation?

And how you will leave in the middle of supper and birth-day parties and bedtime to run calls?

Hmm?

(I know. After that barrage, you are already on his side.) I am always at my best when the unexpected crops up. Especially when armed with a hundred arrows to shoot its direction. They look a lot like question marks, and there's more where those came from.

What about ME*? Being your most important person?*

Now here is a curious thing. My husband, who is gentle, wise, compassionate, and devoted to me, listens patiently on this issue, hears me out, offers precious little in the way of defense or comment, and then goes out and does whatever he wants with the fire department.

I have never experienced anything like it. Most decisions we hash out together. Most times, if I care enough and throw my weight in hard, I can swing the ship. This time, at the end of every conversation with him I run up against the unmoving rock of his silent resolve.

He acknowledges my feelings. And keeps pursuing it. He won't fight for it. He won't explain it, defend it, tell me why he is doing it. But our plans fly out the window every time some nearby cook burns her dinner to a crisp and sets the fire alarms jangling, and every time a stout man down the road falls off his bed and needs a lift assist.

Again and again, I must move forward while missing him. Parent alone. Host our invited guests without him. Share him with everyone else. Make excuses for him. Get all ugly and tight-mouthed, and then make up with him. Again and again.

Worse, he confesses to me that he is not all mine with his eyes and his mind. He fights a recurring battle against lust and illicit images, which shreds my worth before my eyes.

That young woman on the beach in the sunset did not consider that there might be times when she is no longer the sun-moon-and-stars who reigns shining over all and pulls at his heart in ever deepening rhythms. There might be times in all this ministering and sinning of his when she longs for her husband and he is not there.

I am not the center of his universe, and he is not all that I need.

When I am a child, I soak up friendship from the oceans around me, and rain it back down. Girlish secrets and whisperings in church, squeezing each other's hands in code, haymow sleepovers, danger and drama and always on the lookout for boys (who are fascinating, but not to be trusted). We compare notes on life's big questions, like *Is the handsome one looking our way?* We baby our cats and catch handfuls of frogs. We bake together, a simple cake that flops because we are too busy talking. Innocence and harmony. Her headbands in my hair, my book on her nightstand.

When I turn eleven, I leave the uncomplicated life, the woodsy forts and make-believes and snowball fights, the dolls I still play with, the guileless joy. I move a thousand miles from my old life to a community that might as well be a caricature somebody drew up, Least Like Previous Place of Residence. I cannot learn the language. The girls my age trash-talk each other affectionately, get excited about pro football season, use guilty terms I've never heard, stalk the cute boys, and rebel behind their parents' backs. I am always missing the cue that huddles ten heads close together to whisper secrets, and leaves one upright on the outside. At one disastrous birthday party to which I am invited, my new friends exhibit behaviors I have never imagined: taunting a father's employee with fingers in ears and tongues stuck out, throwing food at each other in a deli, and talking about someone who *had sex*. My mother has instructed me about *sexual intercourse*, but I didn't know there was anything about it to be *had*.

I am so lost as to be dirt beneath their feet, a hopeless goody two-shoes in a world of mutineers. I can't find my way in. For years, my friendships hold tenuously to the misfits and outsiders and transplants in the community. I catch lifelines from friends I make in other places, with whom I feel the indefinable spark of connection that cannot be replicated or explained. We swap letters by the bucketful, phone calls, whispered confessions of first boy-love, tears, pressed flowers, funny stories.

When I marry, I move to a neighborhood where I know no one but my husband, and once more I begin again. The local loneliness is paralyzing as I try to fill relational hunger with one man and long-distance girlfriends. The latter I am already somewhat accustomed to. But as I birth my children and put down roots, something about mothering pushes me hard toward regional relationship. Am I less able to meet my own needs when I am meeting the needs of small humans? Or does it simply mean more and matter more, the plugging in and connecting? Or am I discovering the inadequacy of any one relationship to satisfy heart hunger? I can nibble every bit of meat off those bones and feel guilty for my greed, and still want more.

I grow hungry for local friends, women close enough to pop over with a new recipe or some extra morning glory seeds, to celebrate my baby's tiny milestones and reciprocate with their own stories of first teeth and toddling steps. People to know me. Here.

No one in my new community jumps out at me, sparks the spark, forms the instant superglue connection I am familiar with. Besides, I am now in the married-woman category, placed in groups and paired in responsibilities with women twice and three times my age. They get together to clean houses, and their conversations involve the garden yields of the season and Christmas cookie recipes and hemorrhoids.

I am longing for a bestie, someone who instantly clicks with me. My husband says, *Maybe you will have to find a different way. What does friendship look like to her? Maybe it looks like swapping babysitting, talking about green beans, sharing tips for cleaning sinks. Maybe it's more practical. Let it be what it is.*

And so I do. I learn how to build friendships all over again, from scratch.

I talk about diaper rashes and learn to team-pick strawberries with a friend who lives near me. I do not understand her, and her jokes intimidate me, and her easy mothering times multiple children baffles me. But she hangs in there with me when I am presenting an image of perfection instead of a real live woman. She makes good milkshakes and invites us over for Sunday dinner, and our children play. Before long, we are pastor's wifing together, and we discuss congregational issues.

One day we sign up for an overnight trip to a conference for women in ministry. This stretches me. What will we talk about, all the way there? Will my pajamas look okay? I miss a turn on the way there, and it adds thirty or forty minutes to our already lengthy drive. We get to see sunrise over Pittsburgh—that is the redeeming factor—and she is relaxed about it all. We find plenty to say.

The conference turns out to be a deep one, both of us plunging into unexpected emotion regarding identity and soul places and personal worth and our views of God the Father. Into the broken places, loving service is poured: delightful meals we don't have to cook, time to rest and journal and chat, candles, a formal tea party with live piano music, waiters in black and white, rose petals strewn down the hallway.

Late that night, when the conference ends and our emotions are wrung out, we drive half an hour to the place where we will be spending the night. Our road is a crazy one, with more height variance, switchbacks, tummy ticklers, and curlicues than you would believe possible. While I am navigating this, her husband calls. She answers and tries explaining where we are, what we are doing. He mishears something and it cracks us both up. She begins to laugh and then to giggle helplessly, hanging on to that phone and unable to speak. He gets a little stern with her, which is even funnier. I am trying to laugh quietly so he doesn't think he sent his wife out of town with a crazy woman, but I am sharing my silly side with her for the first time and it is too good to be true, this connecting. The vehicle turns completely silent except for our gasps for air.

I am holding on to the steering wheel driving the curvingest road in my state at high speeds, and I am laughing so hard I cannot see the lanes through my tears. We will probably die on this trip, and neither of us seems to care.

I need more from my husband. I need hope for my second son. We take turns being optimistic and discouraged about our ability to parent this particular human. We disagree about methods. Are we being too hard on him or too lenient? What does he need? What do we need in order to do well?

Every date night becomes overshadowed by our discussions about him. He is the mile marker of our progress, the wedge between us, the glue holding us to the same goals. We fight hard, bicker and fault-find and pray. I tell my husband too often what I am certain we need from him.

There comes a time when my husband hits an anger with our son that does not fade. This child (and perhaps his mother) asks for more from him than he feels he has to give, breaks too many competencies, and he turns grim and disconnected toward that son alone.

He doesn't have anything more to give.

The fire department is an easy place to feel like a success.

She will become a life friend, our relationship cemented that weekend. We will learn more of each other. I will remember where I was when she shared the news of each of her seven pregnancies with me. We will share evenings corralling our children while our husbands meet, splash dates in her backyard, and melting popsicles. We will keep the road warm between our houses, stopping in for coffee and bringing each other meals after babies. Her signature homemade bread. My meatball casserole. Big slabs of cake when a grandparent dies. I'll recognize her handwriting in countless precious notes, her affirmations, her faith for me when I don't have any left. I will love her beautiful eyes, her high-contrast clothes, her impromptu planning, her bull's-eye sense of humor. I will love *her*.

For all the talk about falling in love, and how it will heal your soul and make you happy forever and complete what you lack, I will tell you what is just as powerful and more transformative: sisterhood.

I love my man more than anything. He is strong and giving, handsome, more relationally attuned than most. He makes me laugh and holds me when I'm sad.

But also, I can talk until I am blue and although he will learn what I mean, he will not grok it in the way a girlfriend will with my very first words. Sisters understand each other in a wordless reaching across lines to find our commonality, an unspoken sorority, a team.

My man has the opinion that matters most. He is the axis around which the world spins.

But also, living with him hurts. We disagree on parenting, we miss important opportunities, and we wound each other with our infidelities. I want to be enough for him, I want to be what he needs, and I am never quite enough in my own mind. There is longing and ache. Sister relationships are simpler, not quite as fraught. The world doesn't spin around a single one. There's not as much at stake.

Sisterhood is a call away from shame (I admit my foolish desires and let my faults be known), away from idolatry (marriage should be everything I need), and away from the disastrous self-serving egotism of wanting to be goddess (I long to be the end and the beginning, the trump card, the queen: to own all of one person and wrap him around me). Sisterhood frees me from nonsense.

Having found my way with one friend, I find my way with others. I start with little things: we each have a baby, she wears an outfit I like, we end up on a committee together. Then we go on from there. We laugh hard about a mistake I make, or I ask what it's like having twins and she tells me honestly, or we go on a walk together and the conversation turns real. I try to get free from that eleven-year-old inside my heart who is always on the outside longing to get in. It's easier than it used to be, the way I imagine leaping from a diving board might come to be, though I've never been brave enough for that either. The water bubbling up around my head, the loss of control, the going under rather far, and the trust that this medium can hold me, that I'll come up again. Easier and easier. Farther and deeper.

Friendships with women teach me about relational vulnerability, the hard work of bonding, and the sheer fun of connecting. I learn to make space. There's always a little edge of time that no one else is using. We sneak early Saturday mornings eating breakfast at restaurants, Sunday afternoons while our families nap, and late nights with ice cream on somebody's porch.

Friendships with women offer perpetual presence and novelty, like the omnipresence of God. If one hurts you, another three are there to help you heal.

Relationships are mirrors, held up to our faces by the people around us, who say, *This is what you look like.* I am what other people believe me to be—or so easily, I soon will be. I look at myself in the mirrors they hold up, and I see a goody-goody who doesn't have anything to offer, a person who is more than a little peculiar. First I become it in their minds, and they begin talking to me and acting to me as if I am that person. Then I begin to wonder if that is who I am, and then I begin to believe it, and then, for many years, I am that, at least when I am with them.

I have performed this black magic on others, such as believing my husband to be a sorry no-good derelict who can't do anything right and can't change. He looks at himself in my mirror, and he wonders, and his face begins to change. I believe my sons to be brilliant or freakish, my daughter to be a delight or demand-after-demand-after-demand. They look at themselves, and they wonder.

May the Lord have mercy on the creations of his people. This is not the procreation he had in mind, to reproduce in other people the fallen images of them that we carry in our minds. But it is shockingly effective.

The enchantment for good, thanks be to God, is just as strong. I am influenced by others' faith in me, a powerfully creative tool for good. When I look into the mirror on that snaky mountain road, rounding the brims of the cliffs and hilltops, I see a laughing woman who is a great deal of fun to be with. First, I become it in my friend's mind, and then I become it in my mind, and then I become it more and more in myself. In my turn, I hold up a mirror to my friend, and she sees someone beautiful, fascinating, enjoyable, whose uniqueness is valued and respected.

When I believe my husband to be a man of God, the best thing that ever happened to me, an amazing leader and father in spite of his errors—he becomes what my faith and love tell him he is. When I know my children to be gifts from the Father, precious to Christ, specially crafted for their niche in this world, fully accepted and fully loved, they become what I know them to be.

We cannot create such energy inside ourselves; when we try, our minds close around nothing but fluff, the mass-produced, cheery self-talk of greeting cards. This is why relationships are so damaging and detrimental, and why they are so healing and wholesome—because another human looks into us and says, *I see you, and this is how you look,* and watches us change into what they already know us to be. We are called what we are not yet and brought gradually into its fullness. Relationships reshape identity. Relationships have the power to create different versions of everyone around us.

By experience, I learn a hard thing. Sometimes a relational mirror cracks, especially in my dearest relationships—marriage and mothering. Difficulty warps the image I see, and tells me lies that the person holding the mirror may or may not intend. When an intimate relationship tells me I am inadequate and worthless and nothing and ugly and stuck on the outside, it is essential for me that I find another, truer mirror. Several of them. As many as I can, to encircle me and shine bright rays back into my eyes and tell me I am accepted, one of us, loved, able to be desired. Not to gloss over faults, but to bring my spirit back to truth, and to the person Jesus made me to be.

Do you remember me saying that my son is the mile marker of my progress? That is a warped mirror.

I worry that talking about my husband or children to anyone else is betraying them somehow, exposing what ought not be exposed. Certainly there is a ditch on that side, when I share with the world my whines and grievances. You can ruin a relationship that way. But you can ruin it the opposite way, by not finding the outside support that you need. By failing to seek the restoration you require to return and plug in tighter. By leaning too hard for healing on the source of your conflict. Sometimes you need to hold your tongue and go find a girlfriend.

Girlfriends are the ones who find you crying in the church restroom, who bring you hot soup when you are postpartum, who take care of your babies as well as you can. There is always someone to go to, always a sister. When one is out of town, another will answer her phone. When one is overwhelmed with her own life's struggles, another is fresh from the fight and ready to help.

When my marital mirror distorts badly, one will stay up until midnight listening to my pain.

One will know what it feels like.

One will host a personal photoshoot on her lawn and turn me beautiful again.

One will form her hands into fists and pound them, angry for me, ready to fight. She validates my losses, and then helps me know what to do with them.

One will keep dialing my number, speaking life, letting me be what I am.

One will help me know how to walk forward through the shame.

One will come find me when I am hiding, and give me a hug. Her own body will shake with our crying.

The sisterhood.

There will come a time when I accept being a fire wife, at last. There will come a time when my man becomes the glad and connected father of all our children. A time when he is master of his purity, and mine alone. A time when our souls are knit into undying connection and trust. But it will not come from me hounding him and leeching more—nor from me ignoring the issues and shutting up about them. It will come from him reaching out to men, and me reaching out to women. It will come through the relational magic of generous, faith-filled mirrors.

Is that so naked a posture to have, this needing?

In the days of river rocks (and for many years after), we were strong because Mom and Grandma and Friend and Auntie were just down the road, and we mothered one another's kids and washed laundry together and swapped recipes and gave each other a good ticking off when needed, and got back up and went to shop the market together. We were not above grousing a little about our men, but we went back stronger, more able to lift them up and support them in their imperfect lordship. This is how women handled life and men since the dawn of time.

What would it be like to live in a place where *sister* applies to every woman in your life? A place where you relax into the sorority and know they have your back? You're never marginalized or hung out to dry. Jealousy dissolves into cheering for each other. Loneliness softens into team play, self-interest into empathy, isolation into belonging.

Free babysitting among women is really a thing. Carpooling is simple—if I am going, I pick up her kids. When I forget, she wings it last minute and brings them home. When our kids outgrow their clothes, we pass them to a friend's younger child at no cost. We see each other's houses while they are messy, with kids and Spot and Fluff and Fisher-Price all over the carpet. Our children have to listen to all the mamas, not just their own. If one of them is in trouble, five of us come running.

After we give birth, half a dozen friends show up on different nights with a warm dinner. When we climb into our unlocked vehicles after church, we might find a gift slipped there, homemade cookies or a houseplant. We team up to can dozens of jars of applesauce or to bake for the holidays. We hold impromptu gatherings—*If you're not busy tonight, come over for games and hot drinks. I don't know what we'll eat.*

Without fear of judgment, we talk about the deep stuff. Getting teary in front of each other or laughing till we fall off our chairs is okay, and part of the package. When we confess our sins, we find compassionate faces, solid advice, and warm hugs. I see tears for my griefs running down their faces.

Among all the ways in which my Anabaptist compatriots could grow, like dancing before the Lord and enjoying a little wine now and then, we have this to offer the greater Christian world: a robust understanding of community. To us, *sister in Christ* is not just a pretty phrase. We believe that before God, we are literally of one blood: his family: inseparable: indivisible. One.

My friends and I live this way, and know without doubt we are stronger together.

We have found sorority. We are the sisterhood.

6

LOOKING INSIDE

A few questions for you to consider . . .

1. Who are the girlfriends you can call on anytime, and
   know that they will love you? Who would gladly
   pick up the phone at three in the morning when
   you're in need, even if the two of you haven't connected for a long time? List as many as you can.

2. Do you offer unconditional love to the women in
   your life? How can you tell?

3. Are there particular relationships that you feel
   you cannot share about—or perhaps get help

with—through other relationships? Can you think about why you feel this way? What would help you feel *safe* in seeking help, instead of *disloyal*?

4. When you dream of time with girlfriends, what makes you come alive? Unwinding and cutting loose? Working alongside each other? Intimate understanding? Crazy laughter? Have some fun brainstorming some specific activities you'd most enjoy a partner in.

We know, don't we, that relationships don't always heal? Sometimes they hurt. This we will discuss more in our next chapter.

7

Strangers, Like Me

The Necessity of Speaking Out

———

so

here

is what i

want to know

about heaven—

in a world without tears

how will we ever make sense

of the things we humans did

to one another on earth?

how?

My mother-in-law comes from a bitterly broken childhood. She is raised by a woman who cannot tell truth from fiction, and a series of unprincipled men. As an adolescent, she chooses to leave the abuse and lies and filthiness and run to a safe place. She runs to the Mennonite families who have loved her and her little siblings at summer Bible school. They are solid. They will know what to do.

She finds an anchor there, a father and mother and siblings who take her in and love her to health. When she grows up, her heart is set toward little ones in similar situations. She becomes a foster parent, welcoming a succession of children into her home and adopting one, who becomes my husband's sister. Until the end of her days, her eyes will fill when she encounters a dirty child in need. She gives her time to people with intellectual disabilities, teenagers who can't find a home, and youngsters who need intense physical and medical care. Sometimes the grief of the world rises up in her throat to drown her. But she has a ballast: a stable husband, a good heritage, a big family who loves her. And she doesn't go down. She keeps loving.

My husband, who benefits from her nurture, catches some of her heart. He stays interested in foster care, and brings that interest to our marriage. We discuss it lazily, draped over a couch together, or eating potato casserole in our first year as husband and wife. I have never been interested in foster care. Why? If you want a baby, make one. I listen with curiosity, openness without calling.

I am ashamed to confess one of my main reasons for hesitating: the high chance of failure.

Some fostered and adopted children plug into their new lives, eager for stability, quick to bond. Others, unmoored, spend their lives longing for what used to be, falling back at the earliest opportunity into the lifestyle they are pulled from: the wandering, the isolation, the addiction, the harm.

I need this to work. I want to be a good mom, one whose kids all turn into Sunday school teachers and scientists. How will I know if I can do enough to heal a child? What if she turns away, becomes the high school dropout and the cutter and the druggie and the wild-haired rebel?

Shame.

That is what would happen, and that is what I feel when I admit my questions.

Just as my second son takes a deep dive into behaviors we cannot control or train away, one of my best-loved brothers drives off the rails in his own behaviors and choices. He begins wrecking vehicles, dodging DUIs, stealing money to fuel his addictions. I see the two stories parallel, back to back, the potential for future conduct undermining any kind of parenting, even the best—which I have always felt I've received. The headlines run through my mind.

When Christian Parenting Fails, Chaos Ensues
Child Outcomes Proved to be Anybody's Guess
Worse Than Ever: A Study of Generational Misdeeds

My brother will return to himself and to stability. By faith, I pray my son will. But I don't know how to raise a child better than my parents did. When I look at my son howling on the floor, or throwing a book so hard it cracks our drywall, or sneaking money when I am not looking, I know I can pour twenty anguished years into my boy, one painful day at a time, and he can leave me and go straight to the devil.

This is not the path I planned. If you do A and B, surely C will follow. Decent genes + great love + consistent parenting = a child who can't go wrong.

Newsflash. If free will is a thing, then there is never a guarantee of another person becoming what you envision. They may hate what you love, spit in your face, and abandon all you built into them. This is the risk of loving—the risk of parenting. The risk of *all* parenting.

Only a few years into motherhood, my reputation is already in tatters, my childrearing platitudes gone broke. We will not be the family sitting pretty in the front row of the congregation, all matchies and shining hair and sweet smiles. We will be the family with dark circles under the eyes, one hand firmly on the wrist of a reluctant-participant-would-be-escapee snitching cash out of the offering plate with his free hand. We will be the ones attending church basically for the net gain of teaching our children it is a good idea to go—missing all the good parts, trotting out of the service thirteen times, praying our marriage outlives our parenting. Praying we have something left at the end.

My parenting ideals fall face forward, to smash like an ancient god on the floor of a temple before the glory of the Lord. That is where they belong.

My son may have a devastating future or a brilliant one. He may be good-hearted, savvy, intelligent, compassionate, strong—or cruel, selfish, unregulated, damaging, criminal. For good or ill, he will change the world. That is partly up to Jesus and partly up to me and mostly up to him. But the future has little impact on what I need to do now. First things first: he must survive childhood. The way he will survive childhood is if we allow our crumbling to be seen and get the help and accountability we need. And if we never give up. Parent. Forgive. Speak out. And learn to love for real.

Nothing humbles a soul like loving someone near to you, dear to you, who simply cannot pull his act together and perform. Nothing matches it for teaching compassion and need. The breaking of the heart, the recurring hope and loss, the tears, and the true love born in this place are sacred, and open the heart to loving others.

We call it *empathy*. You can't buy it cheaply in the shops where it's sold. It is the mingling place where hurting meets healing, which enables us to handle more hurting, which enables us to share more healing.

When once I have been wrenched open, I am less frightened by the cracks of others. I am more resilient, more forgiving. Out of my shattered parenting-idolatry grows a passion to love. To love my child with my whole heart, without conditions for success. To love a child who cannot love himself, who can't look ahead enough to see the self-harm his choices will entail, and who can't defend himself on a planet that has proved itself consistently antagonistic toward people who don't fit the mold.

It is my desire to lay myself down around him in a love that he will never be able to shake off, a belonging that embraces him for who he is and not for how he measures up. A love that both releases and holds, that allows the unguarded hours yet never looks away. A love that visualizes the best without demanding it. A love that sees with the good eyes and shines with the good mirror, no matter how many harsh untruths are enacted elsewhere.

It is my desire both to shield and to empower. It is my desire to step between that child and the world and say: This one is mine. Stand back.

Get away from him with your unhelpful sentiments of doom, your labels, your statistics, your judgments, your pseudo solutions, your curled lips, your cold shoulders.

Make a little room for this child who breaks your categories.

Give him a chance, people. Open your hearts. Lend him what he needs.

Reach out a hand to love my small stranger, and find in him a world you cannot imagine: a world of light and wiggles where you have boxes and straight laces. A rippling world of explosive consciousness, an unbounded field of discovery, a heart that knows how to create, how to emote, how to love.

This one is mine. Get out of his way.

When I carve out space for the ones I love, I find in turn that I can breathe more easily. I am kinder to myself and to others. I can allow for an unexpected space of mercy, to be simultaneously imperfect and loved. I tie fewer strings to my love. I risk more. I have less to lose.

Once I fully embrace a person I did not envision, it is not a giant leap for mankind to see that there are more children than mine in the world. Some of them have no one to speak on their behalf. There are many unclaimed strangers in my streets. They are in the aisles of the supermarket, in the government housing blocks, in the school cafeteria line, in the church pews. So near me that I cannot reach out a hand without brushing one of them. So far away. So shut out by prejudices and societal norms that often I do not even see them.

Who will speak for them?

Quite by mistake, I fall in love with a needy child in my town. She is being raised by an aging relative several times removed, while one parent sacks out on the couch and the other leaves town for the West. There is a mean old uncle in the home, and he slaps the child around a bit. I invite her over to play. She plays Wolf with my boys, kneeling on the top bunk and tipping her nose to the sky and howling for joy. What does she need? What can I do for her?

She calls me Mom one night, and I sing "Jesus Loves Me" while I drive her home. Before I close the door of her house behind me as I leave, I hear her begin to cry hard, and I wonder what happens when no one is looking. I hate that I am leaving her there and driving away.

Suddenly, needy children are not an abstract, a thing to be idly discussed over potato casserole. Making another baby does not help this child whom I love in my town. And so one day, we take our naïve and artless faith in our hands and request a fostering information packet.

We know nothing. The first time a pair of licensing agents comes out to our house for an interview, one of them describes the court process and the prospect of reunifying a child with his birth family. She says, *It can go either way. Whatever the Master decides.*

I am taken by her fascinating hat tip to Christ. It is many weeks before my moment of revelation dawns. *Oh. Juvenile court master.*

Okay then. We are as green as the garden.

In the October that begins our twelfth year of marriage, we receive a nonverbal child in the name of Christ. He is four years old, with Angelman syndrome, a chromosomal abnormality that makes him a large and happy baby. I have dreamed of welcoming someone else's baby in need; it didn't cross my mind that he might be four.

I hold him on my hip that first night, getting used to him while his caseworker runs over hasty and relevant details of his case. *What does he understand of what you are saying?* I ask.

She looks at me. *Nothing.*

His eyes are as crystal as the sky, and as empty. Even when he looks at me, he isn't really looking. He smells of cigarette smoke and a wet diaper and drool. He is like a living body without a resident.

He won't fall off the couch, but he also can't get off it. Can't climb steps. Can't eat from a spoon. Refuses to drink anything in his bottle but children's dietary supplement, six or eight cans a day. Wears a diaper. Takes daily medication for seizures. Doesn't know what a toy is, does not reach to play.

How to connect with him? When I lift him for his first bath (which he loves), he laughs compulsively. *I think he's terribly ticklish,* I tell my husband. Then we search the internet for Angelman syndrome.

Mental disability. Developmental delay. Problems with balance and movement. Severe speech impairment. Frequent smiling and laughter. Epilepsy. Drooling. Formerly called happy puppet syndrome for the sweet temperament and jerky movements. Fascination with water.

How can I tell you how dear he is, and how off-putting? How easy he is, and how hard? Am I sure I can lovingly nurture without conditions?

On his first night in our home, he wakes us in the darkness with an awful racket, wailing and shouting, standing up against the cribside and shaking the whole bed about. I run to him. *Honey, it's okay. I'm right here.* He puts his finger in his mouth, a trademark gesture we will learn to recognize, and howls around it.

Do you know what keening is? I ask my husband. *I think it's his version of keening.* He's grieving in the only way he knows, the high-pitched wailing cry of someone who has lost it all. What have we done to this child by uprooting him?

We watch him bloom in our house, his face turning up to the light. We submit to his aggressive bonding, slobbery hands on our faces and in our hair, unmanaged arms around us. He gets off the couch one day. He sits and rocks on our floor, and soon pulls himself up by the furniture and takes steps along it. He comes when we hold out our arms. He reaches to touch our faces, and he begins to play with toys and get into mischief and take tumbles from his explorations. He begins to be comforted by our love. Occasionally, he looks into our eyes. He holds hands with my daughter when she takes his in her own: two four-year-olds joined in a place beyond words. He begins to take lurching steps forward with two hands held, and then one. He climbs the stairs and sits moaning at the top because he doesn't know how to come down. He begs for me with nonverbal imploring when I walk past him.

What does he understand of what you are saying?

More than we will ever know.

Forgive me, Lord, for taking so long to notice: there is a whole personhood contained in him, stuck inside an uncooperative body. A child peers out through the dazzling empty eyes. We call him Angel Boy, and I become his mother.

Everyone tells us how good we are with him, how adaptive to his issues, how he is developing. *Look at him! I'm sure he turned his head when you said his name.*

So I am the good Christian, the brilliant foster mom saving the day, driving up in my snazzy little minivan to drop him off for supervised visits with his birth mom and dad, who apparently are missing key skills here. I find joy in my new role, and I'm pretty good at it I think. I hand him over to Mom, listen to her for a while, smile politely, slip back into my vehicle, and drive away.

Until one day as I duck behind the van door to leave, Mom calls me back. *How's he doing?*

Yeah, Dad says. *We hear some stuff from the caseworker, you know, but we'd like to hear how he's doing from you, you know.*

Oh burn! Slap of the universe on the face of a do-gooder, a zip-in-and-outer, a look-at-me-doing-my-little-charity-act performer.

Oh! I say.

Um, yeah. Well, we've been trying to feed him yogurt off a spoon. He doesn't really like it, but we can usually get a little in and he smacks his lips. I think the strawberry flavor kinda reminds him of his favorite bottle. He really likes my daughter, he crawls over to her when she comes into the room.

Their faces light up.

Forgive me, Lord, for taking so long to notice: there is a whole personhood contained in them. I know it when I start listening for real. When one day I hear in Mom's conversation her son's cry for someone to listen, to talk back. When one day my foster son's eyes look out of his father's face, and I see a secluded child trapped in the body of an adult who still doesn't know how to make it on his own. Their nakedness pierces me. Our children are not the only fringe people struggling to adapt to the requirements of an exacting world.

For the first time, but not for the last, I yearn to take the head of the whole world and hold it against my breast and say, *It's okay. Mommy is here. Shh.*

Who speaks for the fringe people, all those locked into poverty and incomplete education on the sidelines? The welfare people? The addicted and isolated? The beautiful souls looking out of empty eyes? The yellers at children? The adults wandering lost in alternate worlds of dark reality while their little ones wait outside? Who speaks for them? Who defends what they need?

Do you think I am saying *them* and *us*? Those people?

The passion for speaking out dawns in me when they draw me into their circle. When I hear their myriad histories, and all the hidden parts remind me of my own. When I look into their mirror, and see that they are trusting me because they are allowing me to be mistaken and to be one of them, and I realize with a jolt that I am. I have been a welfare person and I have been poor and I have made terrible mistakes with my children and I have been broken beyond recovery. I know myself to be one of those people, the fractured ones.

I have put them in the Needy Box, and walled myself into the Giving Box, so busy saving their child from them that I forgot to see. Is it possible that they have more to give me, in their humility and readiness, than I have to give them?

For the first time, but not for the last, I lay my own head against the breast of the world, and I let myself belong.

Forgive me, Lord, for taking so long to notice: I am one with the human race in its unending condition of need and inadequacy. I reach for help, and I reach to help, and in so doing I take my place in the chain of creatures holding to each other, clinging to Christ.

On court days they sit quietly in their chairs, the gentlest of defendants, listening as their secrets are laid bare, and not answering back. Her head is down, and she tucks a strand of hair behind her ear. His leg is bouncing with nerves, but he is silent. They take the rain of allegations and recommendations, the plans for assessing their own mental well-being and their attachment to their son.

She tells me what she learns, what she will do differently. He admits his confusion, lets a bad word slip and apologizes profusely. We build a bridge with our words, they the better stone-layers, eager to create a roadway between us. They speak for us to the caseworker, tell us how their son is changing, and how happy they are.

One day his mother hugs me. I didn't know we were allowed to do that.

Our Angel Boy returns to his parents after seven months in our home. They confess they didn't know what he was capable of. They needed someone with new eyes and more energy to show them. Gladly they learn, eagerly they take ownership of self-improvement: charts and classes and checkups. They will be the most workable of biological parents. Good ones to learn from for all the rest to come, because I can't kid myself—I have learned far more than they have.

I learn that people who have been broken and dismissed may become the best and kindest friends, for they live in a world beyond arrogance and judgment. I learn that for them (for us), the immaculate and shipshape people at the top are not a natural choice for advocacy. The people up there may have the power, but they don't have the point of view. It is only those who have been knocked off the pedestals, who have felt the unwelcome shattering, *and who are willing to embrace that posture*, that are in a place to bring relational healing to the wounded places of others. To come more humbly, to bend lower, to speak clearer, to melt away the dividers.

And even then, they (we) might need a little kick in the pants. Because we labor under the delusion that in order to help a person fallen into a well, you need to stay tidy at ground level and drop down encouragement and provisions. I learn we do better if we dive in and link both arms, and walk each other slowly up that steep wall.

The advocates in my life who really understand my problems and come shoulder to shoulder with me are those who have been advocated for, who have been forced to climb down the depths of their own need.

I try to speak for the birth parents at the hearing and write an honest report of their endeavors, their changes, their sincere hearts. I speak for their son and his capabilities, his growth. When I arrive in the courtroom, I see to my surprise that Mom and Dad are holding copies of my words in their hands. *I didn't realize you get copies of my report,* I say apologetically. Their lawyer speaks up. *They don't usually. But I just thought this one was so positive, it would do them good to see it, and I shared it with them. I hope you don't mind.*

I speak for this set of parents, but far more, they speak for me. They speak for humans everywhere, speak up for relationships across artificial barriers. They speak for respect and communication. They see a world where the boxes open, and the needers are givers and the givers need. They praise my success without considering how it may reflect on their own. They teach me that we can team-play—that is a thing. That we can state frankly what we seek from others, and the world will not collapse. *We'd like to hear how he's doing from you, you know.*

I am a stranger, and they take me in.

Now I am one of them. Now I belong, and I can no longer drive lightly away.

We meet often after Angel Boy's return home. He knows me, of course. He will know me for years, mashing my hair against his cheek in a tight hug, laughing, touching, crying out in protest when I stand up after greeting him and turn away from his stroller.

Months later, his mother will give me a gift she has made, a vibrant baby quilt pieced for the infant growing in my womb. She wins a prize for it at the county fair. When someday, after a long and painful journey, I finally hold my last birth baby—is she my fourth? my fifth? my seventh, depending how you count? and who's counting?—she will sleep with this quilt every night for years, wrapped in a tribute to love across the lines. A monument to my friendship with a family who is human.

Like me.

7

LOOKING INSIDE

———

Here we will sit in silence together.

What do you feel?

8

Poppy Seed Prayers

The Ability to Grieve Out Loud

PRELUDE
EVER AFTER

————

My love is love   is love

And does not   change with changes

Feelings may turn from pleasure to pain, hope to loss, joy to shame

But the present pain will be exactly equal to the previous pleasure

There shall be   no   diminishing

My heart is riddled with holes

that   will not

fill

Now I will tell you from the beginning about my last birth baby, and my long and painful journey.

But how to begin a story, any story? The problem with backing up to the beginning is that it's hard to know when to stop backing. I pass through months and years of events-that-led-to, fly by the hospital where I was born, and land somewhere just before the book of Genesis, when all things were developing in the heart of God.

Have I mentioned how much my husband and I love kids? From an uncertain new mom, I become a woman in love with children, all children. I am open to birthing them and open to caring for the children of others, and I want another to keep. Initially, we create deliberate space in our family so we can foster. Eventually, we begin to pursue both choices simultaneously—biology and blending—our arms open. Somewhere in this plethora of parenting I begin to feel all Mother Teresa about myself for loving and sheltering a gaggle of needy children, until I realize that I am harassing my sons into turning their socks right side out before tossing them into the laundry hamper so I won't have to touch the nasty sweat and dirt.

This is my little clue that I haven't yet arrived.

In December of our twelfth year of marriage, while Angel Boy is with us, we say yes to a dream opportunity. A newborn girl is coming into foster care. Her older siblings have all been removed from the home, one is being adopted right now, and there is no kin. Would we be willing to take her?

Well, I mean my goodness yes. What is it about a baby? And one so clearly in need of home?

She isn't even born yet, due at Christmastime, and we start counting the days. We set up the crib, buy newborn diapers, and wash the tiny outfits we carefully stored after my daughter outgrew them. We call her Baby Hope until the exciting time we'll learn her birth name.

The days tick by. Her due date comes, and goes.

We begin to worry, and check in with the agency, only to find there has been a terrible miscommunication: she isn't coming to us as a newborn. She has gone home from the hospital with her mom, and if something goes wrong (as it has with all Mom's babies to date), she will come to us.

We never hear of her again.

Will she suffer for this great risk the agency is running? Does she go to join a sibling? Can Mom pull it together, incredibly?

It is hard packing away the diapers and the outfits, taking down the crib. We had wrapped tiny girl shoes in Christmas paper and given them to our children to tell them a new sister was arriving. Now we must tell them there won't be a sister.

When I discover I am pregnant late in January, I have one of those aha moments so frequent in my faith walk, when I try too hard to make sense of the insoluble. So that's why Baby Hope didn't come . . . this is the Lord's plan for us instead. We have waited and prayed for our next child, and startlingly he has arrived, intact and holy, to the haven of my own womb. Elated, we break out the chocolate and the sparkling grape juice, our classic celebration of baby news.

Two days after our joyful discovery, I begin to bleed. I am alone and I stare at that bright, that absurdly bright crimson, and think nothing but NO. This happens to everyone else. Oh help me, Jesus, please not me. Please not this child.

The bleeding continues. We drive to the doctor to confirm. Is there any way this could be a fluke test and a normal cycle? They run their own tests and pull off the gloves and say, *I'm sorry. With three positive pregnancy tests and this amount of bleeding, I think you're losing a baby.*

I can think of many reasons why this twist should not be part of my story. I have had three perfect pregnancies without issues, I love children, I am trying to honor the Lord and follow his desires in opening both my body and my heart, I have enough sorrow already. But no reason can explain why my womb is empty and my heart is not whole anymore. It simply is this way, and the heavens are silent. Are there to be no protections for those who walk in Christ? No protections for the lives of their children?

Someone I love is irretrievably gone, passed clean out of this world into another where I cannot follow. I trust in my body to do what it knows, what it has done before. I trust in my body to be a good mother, and my own body which I trust betrays me, drops a precious thing I intend to carry, drops it down down down.

Where is he? Please tell me he is not lost and cold in the pipes and the drainage. Please wrap him, Lord. Please let him be a gift in a circle, from your heart to my body straight home to your heart.

Only two days of knowing of him, and never to see and never to touch. I would like to be the kind of mother who could move on and merrily pin her stakes on next month (do such mothers exist?), but I am not. There may be any number of others, but there will never be this one. He is gone.

This winter is a killer: a loss that will cut my heart for years, an irreplaceable I cannot forget. This baby we will never see we name Baby Jesse, the name we picked for my daughter if she had been a boy.

But the losses aren't over. In March, I drive back to the doctor with a painful urinary infection. She says, *Are you pregnant?*

I don't think so, I answer. *I had the miscarriage five or six weeks ago and nothing since.*

I make it all three blocks to the pharmacy before my phone rings. There is a supremely kind nurse on the line. *Honey, after you left the office, we ran a pregnancy test on your specimen, and it was a faint positive. Please don't worry, you're very early on and the medicine we prescribed is safe. Just wait a week and take another test to make sure . . . Are you still there?*

I am there. Only unable to speak.

Within a few days it becomes clear that the baby, if she is there, is leaving my body. Could my hCG levels still be off from my first miscarriage? Could the infection have skewed the test results? Or worse, terminated the pregnancy? I rest my head on my husband's chest and feel the good draining out of the world. Who is God, and why is he not being kind to us?

I ask, *Could we call her Baby Faith?* We are getting good at picking names and genders. This one hat-tips our uncertainty, and the weightier doubt I feel growing within me, a knot of treachery, of undeveloped anger, of loose ends I did not want to find, tied to me by a cord of longing. Fiercely, despairingly, I want my babies, though they are the size of poppy seeds: minuscule, unformed, perfect. We name this child for what I want to hang on to, and for what I feel slipping through my fingers.

In the months to come, I walk and cannot see where my feet are falling.

In my mind, I tell myself the Lord can do no wrong, while simultaneously in my heart, I taste the knowledge that he has betrayed me, lured me into hopes that dissolve before my eyes. Perhaps he is good in some cosmic sense, like a chess player sacrificing a pawn to save a bishop, lofty and unfeeling, performing moves that future generations will label *for the undoubted benefit of all.* But I am not a future generation, I am the pawn. And he is not who I've always thought him to be.

I cry into my pillow. I cry with a baby blanket pressed against my cheek. One day I stitch three of them, just a few inches square, one with the name Hope embroidered in the corner, one Jesse, one Faith. I hold them against my face to absorb the water. Then I get out of my bed and fix the breakfast.

(Do not think too highly of me. It is usually cereal from a box. The rare egg or pancake.)

I know a sure way to drive the grief deep into my story for the rest of my life: to paste it over with nice little things that everyone says, and no one but the most foolish of all means. *God must have something better in mind. You'll have another. Don't cry. Maybe something was wrong with him.*

Grief is a river, and the only way across it is through. Some find a little boat of faith to skim over with. They make it, but never talk much about the water afterward. They are always tucking their feet up, always sitting tight on the boat. *I'm sure it was for the best. His ways are higher than our ways.* I let the ripples meet over my head and feel the sinking, the fading, and hope I will rise. Grief is a river, and the only way I know to get across is to flounder through. Some drown trying.

Who is the God watching all this turbulence? Why is my boat floating uselessly beside me, full of holes? I grab at it and it goes under with me. When I come up for air I yell, and I find it makes me stronger. It grows my lungs big and fills them with oxygen and resilience. Sometimes I have words and sometimes not, but it does not take many words to grieve out loud.

I will die if I do not come to him, and I cannot come any way but howling.

So I cry at him.

I break my years of silent acquiescence to the plans of an inexplicable God.

I protest the cruelty of a broken world, a world where babies do not make it to term. I scream at the God who allows it. I whimper in the darkness when no one else is awake. I learn to wail like David, a song I never hoped to sing. *My son, oh my son, my son.* The grief cracks open above my head and I push my face through to breathe.

I bring God the voice of my grief, and find he can handle it. I find he can handle any voice I bring to him honestly. I find I would rather be Job, shouting at the sky, than Jonah, hiding out in the cargo heading as far from the deity as he can get, heading straight toward a fish that is going to help him find his words again, even if it takes three days and three nights. I would rather be Esther, showing up in the court with my request if it kills me. I would rather be Jacob, clutching a God who won't explain himself, and Gideon. *Pardon me, my lord, but if the* LORD *is with us, why has all this happened to us? Where are all his wonders?* (Judges 6:13 NIV).

I am awash in a grief that could kill me. I would rather cry out for the knowledge of him. I would rather be vocal, and come near. I would rather be keening.

And so I stop censoring the words and emotions he already sees inside me. I learn this: any amount of angry conversation with God is better than any amount of compliance with my back turned. I come to him. I promise to trust him. I commit myself to his worship. But I bring it all.

The avoidance of our grief, inadequacy, and failure is why so many of us are dead inside from the harms of the world. We only know how to bring him our successes and our victories— or our sins. We cannot bring our unabridged selves to him, our forbidden feelings, our hopeless wrestling, our hole-ridden faith. We do not believe that even he can put us back together.

Cementing my grief over with the looking-good, I-dare-not-crack platitudes will not bring me into his presence. But also, I cannot assess the sincerity of those who utter platitudes, because I find that their simple statements, to which I come back dripping and exhausted on the other side of the river, sound completely different there than when spoken dry. *Jesus loves me, this I know.* I can't tell if another soul is wet or dry, except sometimes by the shade of her eyes. Sometimes I get a glimpse of how deep the river was.

I find this also. Speaking the best truths I know in the middle of the river, in the middle of the grief cries, shrieking them if I have to, gives me oxygen to breathe. *I know you are good. Your ways are higher than mine. What are you doing to me? You are the Christ, the Son of God. I beg you, show me who you are.*

To be honest, I rarely find God when I scream into the sky, though I have done this many times in my life, but afterward, when my grief and outrage are spent and I am blown wide open, when I turn in despair at his silence to find he is at my elbow, in the river with me. Afterward is where I find him. He is always quiet then, and his eyes are steady. He is soaked through, and I cannot tell if it is river water or tears on his face, but it is all one.

I lost my Son too. I love more children than I can keep.

He is not up there somewhere dealing out pain to humanity. He is here in flesh at the grave, weeping, ready to speak the resurrection words.

He and I are human, woundable. Not immune to suffering, not held in a bubble of calm in a world of injustice, but allowed to pass through anguish. Belonging to the Father does not spare either of us the greatest of sorrow.

One day I take three seeds from my spice drawer, three black poppy seeds, delicate curled shapes that will never grow, and I dig a tiny hole in my herb bed between the bee balm and the Russian sage. I smooth them over and tuck them in. *Hope. Jesse. Faith.*

The most important survival technique for me becomes getting the mourning out. Cracking open the heart to release the anger, the confusion, the pain. Handing it to a friend and asking, *Would you please help me carry it?* Standing at my kitchen counter when I am utterly alone and saying the words of heresy to him, a whisper and a wail. *I have no idea what you are doing. I don't feel like you are being nice to me. Are you even listening?* Weaving it into a playlist, the rage and turmoil swirling in a safe place, in the music itself, to which I can listen in the quiet evening of my living room and feel it all without going down, because it is outside me.

Clearly God is shutting the door to a new child, and I understand now that I must learn a lesson or pass a test or arrive at a perfect state of surrender before he will grant me this gift. But on a Sunday morning in April, while I am still shockingly human and much mistaken, I find myself looking at the brightest, clearest, most beautiful twin blue lines I've ever seen. I am pregnant again. And I begin waiting for the bleeding to start.

But it doesn't.

And it still doesn't.

And the next day it doesn't too.

For three weeks, I cannot bring myself even to write the news in my journal. I don't dare. At last, I buy the bottle of sparkling grape juice, but I do not drink it yet, and I begin (begin) to hope.

Three days after I write the small and hopeful words, my husband's phone buzzes with an incoming call from Children and Youth Services, and on its heels I receive another from our caseworker. Both are asking the same thing. *There's a set of four siblings coming into care today. Who can you take? Two of them are twin girls, a year and a half old. Could you take one of them?*

Our Angel Boy is still with us, but is due for a successful return to his birth parents within the week. *No,* we say. *Twins need to stay together. We'll take both.*

So it happens that on Mother's Day of our twelfth year of marriage, we publicly announce a healthy pregnancy, spend our last day fostering Angel Boy, and take our toddler twins to church for the first time, alongside three precious biological kiddos.

One twin is strawberry blond, one black-eyed and -haired. They are little penguins waddling on their flippers to a new ice floe. Their eyes are nearly as empty as Angel Boy's, looking upon a strangely colored world without emotion or curiosity. Smart as whips, but environmentally delayed and nearly nonverbal. I lay them in a crib together for their first nap, and they fall asleep on their backs with their hands up and their knees out, in identical interlocking postures. When they awake, they scarf prodigious amounts of food and yell wordlessly for more, churn out unprecedented amounts of dirty diapers.

This is one way that God restores me, by packing my hands and heart so full that I have to live my healing instead of thinking it through. I find redemption in the clinging of small hands on the outside of me, and the precious tap-dancing of tiny feet on the inside. God has given me three babies to love for the three I grieved, without an insurance policy on any of it. Any week could bring the losing.

I find myself cleaning bathrooms after the children are in bed at night, after working myself silly caring for them all day. Toys perpetually litter my floors, along with a whisk attachment from my mixer, a granola bar wrapper, board books, a smartphone that is always off-limits for toddlers, somebody's socks, fifteen tissues pulled from the box, and grainy crumbs from the last two meals. I tidy up late at night and I fall into bed, drained, thinking, *How can I keep them? How can I ever give them up?*

And then, several weeks after accepting the twins, we meet up with their birth parents for a family team meeting. Everyone is kind and civil while plans are discussed. At one point, a twin toddles off toward the exit and her birth mom uses her full name.

Lilly Hope! she warns.

Hope? I say, surprised. *Is that her middle name?*

Yeah. We had their first names picked out long before, but their middle names we picked at random right after they were born. That one is Hope, and that one's Faith.

I knew Christ was with me in the river.

The problem with ending a story, any story, is that I'm not at the end yet.

In search of it I pass in forethought through months and years of events-that-might-come, and land not only in a quiet grass plot where I will lay my body down, but somewhere beyond the book of Revelation, when the things I have entrusted to the Son of God are returned with interest. We are still living without a guarantee of anything but his presence.

But I have come to have a poppy seed–sized faith, and another of hope, and another of pure need, that this process plays a significant part in God's economy—for human love and loss to bring many griefs and countless children against his chest: miscarried, fostered, birthed, beloved. Bits of my heart walk around my city, and around eternity.

This is the story of my grief to date, and speaking it aloud is the only way I can survive not only what is past, but what is about to come.

8

LOOKING INSIDE

Will you trust God enough to give him the parts of your heart that are unhealed?

Sometimes, writing what you feel is simpler than speaking it, and starts you on the same journey toward greater honesty with a Father who already knows you intimately. See if you can find words without censoring them, for once. But do not forget to tell him the best truths you know.

Scream, if you need to. Cry. Beat on his chest.

He wants all of you. It will be okay.

9

Negatory

The Cost of Owning No

PRELUDE
SILENCE

___

S ometimes I think I am the only one with more questions
than answers and
I wonder how it feels to be sure of things
L ike refugee solutions and warming oceans and the mis-
sion of the church and why babies are stillborn. I
E nvy those who have many ideas to share and I remember
the days when I did too but
N ow I have more tears than thoughts, and when I read Paul
I'm not even sure I'm permitted to speak, in
C ase I am being a rebel woman and usurper, but whether I
read him well or not, I have just enough
E nergy for living and none at all to fight.

brew myself a cup of tea, not quite spiced enough or sweet enough, because of not wanting to be the kind of person who lives to excess. My tea bag dangles above my mug, dripping off. There is probably some significance in the fact that it is rotating slowly counterclockwise, if only I knew what it was. I must go against the flow? The smoke detector batteries around the house need changing: start in the southwest corner and go backward around the perimeter? Well. If the universe wants to give direction, it will need to be more specific.

The words need to come out and my fingers are itching to press the right buttons, to capture the thoughts. So little time. So much taco meat to cook for dinner. So much running of different people different places. So many paper towels and hair elastics and soup crackers to buy in town.

I inhabit a culture of traditional and time-honored values. Where I come from, married women do not perform the work of the mind. We perform the work of the body. We are talented in the laundry room and brilliant in the kitchen. We are good at making beautiful babies and dressing them well. We are supremely capable with dirty windows. Our big thinking we outsource to our husbands and our community.

This may not be the best way to become whole people. Yet I suppose it could be. On the one hand, leaning overmuch on others stunts personal growth, development, and opportunity. On the other, some experience the intentional formation of the heart, and the safety, as pure gift. How many women in this age are given the luxury of trust in the judgment of their lovers and the care of their leaders?

In their turn, our men lean for wisdom on each other, and so the community builds on itself and leans into the keystone, the serving Christ whose humility and goodness we attempt to emulate.

Serving is what we have been trained for.

By contrast, today's wider world prizes individualism and self-actualization, particularly for women who are emerging from a system of male dominance. I am full of empathy. But the solutions they're bringing us aren't working.

I may have one foot in each of two cultures, but instead of seeing the differences I see the similarities. Whether women are *expected to serve* the world or *empowered to change* the world, there is a common thread of a whole lot of effort going on here, a highly motivated attempt to carve out a place for ourselves, to do all-that-and-then-some, to earn a worth we have not been given—and to do it by ourselves.

Those who pull off the highest performance are rewarded. So we work that treadmill harder and faster. We say yes to everything. Some of us say yes because we are obedient helpers, and some because we are driven reformers, but we all say yes, a lot.

I have worked for years to be seen as a yes person. Yes, I will babysit your child. Yes, I will donate food to your grocery drive. Yes, I will fill that role on the church roster. Yes, I can pick up your child along with mine. Yes, I will sing in the community choir. Yes, of course I will accept a challenging foster placement.

Everybody likes the yessers, because they help the system work and because they look good on the annual report. Look what we've accomplished! Virtues like optimism and activism and initiative and energy are king. The slogan of the day is *Believe in your yes, and go for it against all odds.* Don't let anyone tell you no or hold you back. If you can dream it, you can do it. The people who say no, even the people who accept no, are blacklisted as the ones who can't handle it, the negative nancies, the naysayers and doubters and downtalkers.

We want permission to push our limits hard, and we don't even question whether we're being pushed into pushing ourselves. Who is setting this standard? Our modern success stories, our legends, our movies, brim with yes. Today's favorite hero, from Hollywood to cutting-edge Christendom, is the stubborn young girl who won't take no. By defying her own limits and the wisdom of everyone around her (parents, authorities, and every known convention), she epically conquers the world and defeats the enemy. All the people come crawling to acknowledge that she was right and she had what it took. She makes her own reality, and she says yes. Atta girl.

I guess trusting your people and acknowledging inability aren't virtues for women anymore?

Where I come from, we reject egotism and defiance as paths to world-healing, though sometimes that means we lack motivation to bloom in the ways we should. I dream of a day when humans are free to embrace both pieces: what we are made to be and what we are not—what we don't need to be.

Where are the hero stories of the people who said no?

My life burgeons into constant childcare, twenty-four seven. I have said a delighted yes. We have five children, not counting the unborn one squirming against my ribs, and the oldest is just turning ten.

The lovable twins we took into our hearts are what well-meaning people call *a handful*. When not watched, they discover the water dispenser in my fridge and splash lakes of liquid over the vinyl floor. The entire kitchen is waterlogged by the time I appear.

Are they all yours?

Outdoors, they find a mud puddle I thought had dried up. Do they roll in it? Sweet dresses are crusted with earth. Streaks trail down their arms and faces. There is a lump of grit and grass clippings in one's hair, where the other deposited it with a soft cupped hand. Plop.

Oh, lady, you have your hands full.

One twin sits sideways in her high chair, working on the fifth bowel movement of the day. It squishes out of her diaper onto her cloth chair and strap. When I lift her out, she steps in it, and in less time than it takes to tell, a mess is on both feet and the floor. This will be her second bath of the day.

Just enjoy them while they're young, they grow up so fast.

While I work with my second son, who is roaring like a bull in his bedroom over some Lego incident with his brother, the twins find my husband's cologne and slather it joyfully about. Why am I always appearing too late? *Self-resolution and experiment are part of healthy child development.* They reek like little men. Little penguin men, and I fill the bathtub once more.

You know what causes this, don't you? Wink.

Each Tuesday, a play-and-speech therapist comes to sit in an easy chair and take an hour and a half to tell me what a good job I am doing with the girls. We have investigatory medical appointments, agency check-ins, court dates, and parental visits twice a week—if the parentals appear.

I miss the days when all my kids were little. We could stay home all the time, no one put pressure on us to do any-thing extra.

I buy groceries by the barrelful, water the houseplants that have not yet been shredded by small hands, and make eleven quarts of homemade blueberry jam at nine o'clock in

the evening, because that is the only time I can get it done.
One evening after dinner, I require my older children to help
me weed flower beds until seven o'clock, and my husband
gets called to a motor vehicle accident and my son sets the
clock half an hour ahead so he can get to the creek earlier. The
babies cry.

Is this one yours too? Where do you gather all these children?

Every moment my work is laid before my eyes: clear:
urgent: unavoidable: more than I can do.

I am Mother Teresa run ragged, snapping at my precious,
hard-won, longed-for children, the darlings, the dumplings
with mud in their hair and snot running in streams from their
nose holes and cat scratches on their arms from lugging the
kitties in a chokehold. My belly grows round and ponderous.

Every morning we are immaculate. Our house is tidy for
a few moments, and our hair is combed adorably with little
bows, and we are all dressed and sane. Then a twin starts biting: four people in one day to the point of blood, and what
consequence can I give her when I have signed a document
prohibiting corporal punishment?

No. I say firmly. *No.* In this world of yeses, here is a firm
negative. *We do not do that in this family.*

In her innocent stubborn face I see the trump card. *Technically, oh foster mother mine, we do. Raarr.*

How can I possibly keep them? How can I ever give
them up?

The twins still have about two words apiece (not that their
therapist is trying, though this mama is); they cry far more than
most children almost two. We teach them a handful of basic
signs. They giggle and invent telepathic games with each other,
sisters always in tune, feelers always out. They trust everybody
and commit themselves to no one, schmooze with strangers,

smile their adorable dimple-chin grins, eat compulsively, howl their preferences. They want every drop of our attention, act out instantly when we give some to another child, or even to each other as husband and wife. And they cry and cry. They are emotionally starving, and all the love in the world cannot fill that black hole.

They play a game we call Pushmi-Pullyu, after Dr. Dolittle's famous animal. One twin signs for a drink, and I bring it, but it is in the wrong color of sippy cup and so she arches in her high chair and bursts into every sign of a broken heart. By now her sister is signing for one as well, so I pass the cup to her. She does not want it, because it was offered first to her sister, but I do not bend and she begins to drink, leading to a full-blown hissy fit by the first twin, who now needs the cup as Gollum needs the ring, screaming and lunging against her straps across the great void between them—all of two feet, but you'd never know from watching. When the second twin is done drinking, I offer the cup back to the first. But now I have done it all wrong. She takes it in her pudgy fist without a taste, her face a fury of toddler rage, and wings it at me. I pick the cup off the floor and rub my arm and set the rejected vessel on the table, out of reach. She sees the finality in the gesture and melts down completely, because she is thirsty and she wants it. Throws her spoon at me too, and her dish, with its remnants of macaroni.

This is the Pushmi-Pullyu game: when we offer a gift, the girls do not want it, and when it passes out of their reach, they must have it. They are two-year-old magistrates with the principles of vixens.

I love these children from my heart. Also, I live for their naptimes.

I bake ten loaves of homemade bread for kids' club at church. I keep after the laundry. I sew maternity clothes for myself, and a special birthday dress for my daughter, who is turning five. I pull my hand off my husband's knee because a twin is screeching at me to remove it; *she's* sitting on his lap. I spend a morning mending books. We have too many torn pages, broken dishes, and spilled liquids to count.

Where is my community? Who is going to help me raise these children here? What if I don't have enough energy left when the time comes to bring this baby into the world?

The twins may leave soon. Perhaps before the baby. Their birth family hovers on the edge of functional home life. What counts as a home? What counts as a life?

My second son's behavior always frays in the summer. I cannot possibly give him enough structure, despite our charts and schedules and chore lists and fun. He needs moment-to-moment direction, activity, watchfulness. This summer, his proclivity for rule-breaking reaches a new high. His charisma and humor make me laugh every day, and in between he belittles his sister, shoots looks of hatred, rages around the house.

One day, they call a Code Adam for my daughter in a department store, because I cannot find her anywhere and I am starting to panic. It is August and we are school shopping while my husband keeps the twins. My boys, who are eight and ten, are selecting a cartful of great gear and I scold my five-year-old daughter for distracting, begging, whining, and when my back is turned she slips away and hides. I do not know that. I only know she is gone, nowhere to be found in the aisles around us. I ask a store associate for help and she speaks into her radio. She asks what my daughter is wearing, how old she is. It is when she says *Check the bathrooms* that my heart turns cold. I watch the workers mobilize, moving slow and steady, checking, seeking. It is many moments before one finds her. Only her little skirt ruffle is hanging out from beneath a women's clothing rack, just a few steps away from the back-to-school section. Then I take her in my arms and we cry hard and when I pull back to look at her, her lip is quivering, and the associates are wiping their eyes. I can hardly speak my thank you to them past the fear and gratitude in my throat.

What am I doing? Who am I missing? What child is not getting enough from her mother?

At night I have recurring dreams of standing last in the food line, after all the dishes are emptied down to the scrapings. I dream of packing enormous amounts of clothes, always one more thing to remember and fold neatly and add to the stack. I dream of being unable to leave in time, of running out of supplies, of climbing a long steep hill to nothing, my belly too heavy.

I am hungry.

If happiness is wanting what you have, I should be the happiest woman in the world.

I wonder what it means to be thankful in the middle of a messy life. I am thankful, but I am not always content. Are they the same thing? How do you love the life you have while plugging like a workhorse to make it a little better? I don't mean to make more money or to take nicer vacations. I mean to cook a special dinner, to breathe in a moment of silence, to have a kitchen floor that is reasonably clean, to raise children who know how to work hard and play well and clean things up.

My fourth newborn comes to my arms at Christmastime in our thirteenth year of marriage, while the twinkle lights shine on my banister and the berries are red. I now have six children ten years old and under. Two sons, two daughters, two foster daughters. I swirl in wonder around my infant on this silent night, and she sleeps her way through the noisy day, her perfect poochie lip tucked down. I sleep her on my chest, keep her within reach.

We have arranged one week of respite care for the twins in another home: enough time to recover strength and bond with the baby. Everyone tells us to take longer, but we will not give up children for convenience, like changeable décor. I want them with me if I can. People do not understand this.

When they return for a visit partway through the week, they pull away from me toward their babysitter, and tantrum when I take them into my arms. They have been with us for seven months, away for four days. They are two girls unmoored and unattached, bent by forces beyond their control. They have developed head colds, coughs and drainage and a huzzah party of germs sneezed onto my newborn.

I cannot do this.

I who am good at loving children, I who take them in as though they are my own, I myself the angel of compassion for lost kids, run smack up against the fact that I forgot what motherlove was until I met it newly born, and I do not have enough of it to go around. How can I care for these two, their smudged faces and stringy hair and loud voices? I forget why they are here. What if they hurt the baby?

(It is a silly fear. They are unfailingly tender to her.)

I am everything to my newborn, and she to me. She is bone of my bones and flesh of my flesh and I love her more than anything I have ever encountered. I want to lose myself in her care. I nuzzle her beautiful skin, dress her, breastfeed her, photograph her. When she cries, I know what she needs. Me. I am the mama, the everything, the enough. She drinks and is full, her face peaceful, her body relaxed. Come here, little darling. Let me wrap you close.

Here, for the first time in life, I become deplorable to myself. I cannot feel what I want to feel. I want to want my twins again, want to keep them. I want to be good at this. I want them to be my daughters again as they were, but the life has drained clean out of this party. I know who my daughters are.

The mighty crash you hear is the sound of me falling from my own pedestal.

What kind of a mother am I?

I pile the guilt inside myself, whispering it only to my husband in the dark of evening, when no one can see.

What kind of woman feels this way?

The twins come home to stay, accustomed to being darlings and celebrities. Their bodies are heftier and their voices more strident than I remembered. Bottomless pits yawn inside them. More food! More time! More touch! More attention! More! More! More! We settle in for a long winter. A teenage friend comes once a week to help me, her energy and sweet spirit a gift.

At home, it works. We shut the doors to the rooms they will trash. We know our work and our limits. When we melt down, it is okay. I can meet the children's needs amply, but then ignore the extracurricular whining, and no one hovers to find out what they want when they themselves do not know.

In the wide world, we have no boundaries. Suddenly two active and hungry girls are unleashed on a generous society. They are cuddled and coddled and endured. Friends are first flattered and then puzzled as my toddlers attach to them, crawl all over their laps, help themselves to their water bottles, change their minds fifty times about up or down, in or out, yes or no. Yes is good. No is better. Oh wait, yes! No! They are two beautiful butterflies with hollow tongues, drinking up intoxicating entertainment and milking it. And oh, the lovely, lovely food . . .

I hear myself intruding, apologizing, always telling people, *Just tell her no*. But it is hard for others to do it; harder still for the girls to have so much temptation and so many minions eager to do their bidding; hardest of all for me to be the mean parent who does not want her child to have good things.

In later years, I will know more about attachment issues than I do now, and I will look back and wish we drew the lines tighter, not looser. *No one feeds them but us. We keep them in our arms in public places. Please do not snuggle her, it is deeply confusing.*

We need to say no. But there is not enough of us to go around.

When are we doing those we love a disservice by pretending we have enough when we don't?

We climb our way back to love, back to the feelings of love through the actions of love: the dressing pretty and the rocking close and the gentle giving, over and over. I plan little tea parties with the twins, and read them stories, and buy them new ribbons to do their hair all cute. We lie on the living room floor in a heap, snuggling and tickling and giggling in our pajamas.

We climb our way back to love just in time to face a question no parent should ever be asked: *Will you keep these children?*

The twins are coming up for adoption. Twelve months of living here is a frightfully long time when you are two and a half years old, and we have a deadline by which we must decide. Yes? Or no?

We do what we know to do: we ask for wisdom from our community, the people we trust most. They say, *How is your family doing?* They say, *We will support you no matter what.* They say, *Your son. What about your son?* They say, *Is there enough? Who is slipping through the cracks?*

We know which children are getting the leftovers. We lie in bed at night and my husband's tears shake us both. I am lost and horrible and alone. We cannot give them up. We cannot keep them.

Sometimes, our fostering agent tells us, *you have to let go of something good so that something better can happen.*

I wonder what good means. I wonder what could be better than us.

We meet with the children's caseworker and we say the word we could never say.

We say no.

We will torture ourselves with this decision for months and years of our long grieving, visiting and revisiting, circling slowly counterclockwise. We come back to the same place each time.

No.

Service is what we know, and what we are raised for. Thinking of others. Being the yes people and the indomitables and the invincibles. Pushing the limits of our endurance. Shining the light out there and praying the in-house needs will take care of themselves.

But we are not stubborn adolescents with a dream, determined to buck the tide and save the world. We are exhausted adults, determined to live within the wisdom of our people.

Far from yes being good and no being bad, the reality of choice is far more complex, interwoven, and inevitable than it appears. Yes and no are inseparable twins, opposite and definitive sides of every decision we make. Hidden in this no is a yes to the children we have already promised to keep. Are we wrong? God forbid that we drop what we have in reaching for more.

We live within a reality of limitation we cannot change or disregard, and we say no.

We do not have to wait long to find out what could be better than us. We are paired with an adoptive family whom we help select—a stable two-parent home with a marriage that has lasted eighteen years childless. A large and generous extended family is waiting to overflow their pent-up love of children onto these girls, to flood, to drench, to heal. We will take our place in that extended family. Our twins will consciously remember only their forever home, but when they are old enough to make sense of their origins, they will tell their parents, *You are our mommy and daddy. But the Zooks gave us our names.*

Technically we did not.

But we don't mind taking credit for a little hope and a little faith.

9

LOOKING INSIDE

———————

I wonder what you think of our story. I imagine I have fallen off your pedestal too.

    1. Which is easier for you to own: yes or no? Why?

    2. How do you know if some question or opportunity deserves a no? Make a list of the criteria that guide you.

3. What is the biggest loss you have sustained through your own deliberate no?

4. How have you forgiven yourself for being what you are—finite?

10

Peanut Butter and Dragon Wings

The Gift of Physicality

There are human experiences that find relief only in the writing of extremely tacky poetry—the kind that Uncle Joe reads aloud at his grandniece's wedding, laboring under the impression that he has produced something clever while everyone else ate cake. ("Her mother and father did her adore, little knowing what lay in store . . .") Thank you for indulging me. I've found there is nothing like a bad rhyme to lift the spirits.

A few years ago we vowed sickness and health
But what that entailed I couldn't have shown ya
The germs staged a coup and attacked us by stealth
The year I had bronchitis and he had pneumonia.

The children were coughing, the fevers were rife.
I said, "Hello, doctor? I thought I would phone ya
Hubby says when he breathes he is stabbed by a knife
I bet I have bronchitis and he has pneumonia."

The comforting thing is that all of this landed
Into the first month of the new year we've known
So the rest can't be worse than the scoop we were handed
When I had bronchitis and he had pneumone.

Unless of course somebody dies and gets buried
Or my mind says, Goodbye pal, it's nice to have known ya
. . . Or a cannibal sharpens his axe to debone ya
. . . Or the orthodox church takes a notion to stone ya
. . . Or the wrecker has an accident right while he's towin' ya
. . . Or a stranger says, Here's a black backpack to loan ya
(KABOOM)
All things considered, I'm just not that worried
Since I had bronchitis and he had pneumonia.

One of the enchanting things they don't tell you about
motherhood ahead of time is how many body fluids will
be involved. I knew there would be diaper contents to clean,

for instance, but I didn't know how many of them would escape to be slap-dashed in various places around my house and on my person. At times I feel my private identity shrinking to the breadth and depth of a tissue. Need one? I'm here. Wipe it on me.

Every orifice of a child is capable of producing something, and all of it must be smeared somewhere. Add in a winter flu season, and you have a recipe for real production.

We go on, stripped of some of the identity that gave us worth, praying that what we are doing matters.

In a bleak January in our fourteenth year of marriage, three weeks of intense coughing by Mrs. Zook develops into one hundred percent of her kiddos sick, including a new foster-baby-for-the-weekend who turns into a foster-baby-for-two-weeks-and-counting. She self-identifies as nocturnal and then begins upchucking violently. I have dealt with many fluids by this time, but never projectile. O ye sofas and carpets, beware. This baby means business.

My washing machine stops working, and several inches of water pool in our basement from days and days of rain. Even the sky cannot stop running unwelcome fluids. No wonder the germs will not die. I get to the place where I can see them, and we cannot shake them off. At my children's school, more kids are staying home sick than coming healthy, and the building closes its doors for a day to let everyone rest. Fever comes to stay with us a while. My baby develops an ear infection. My kids cough. I cough and cannot stop coughing.

My symptoms progress from a throat cough to a chest cough to a barking, breathtaking, unstoppable hacking. I wake in the night unable to breathe, and I sit up panicking, wrestling air into my lungs with a long, painful gasp you can hear in the next room.

There are worse illnesses. A month earlier, my mother is given the Christmas gift of a diagnosis: aggressive breast cancer. Now she receives her first chemo treatment and my sister flies all the way from Israel to spend a month taking care of her, and from my little-fifteen-minute-drive-away I long to support them, be present with them, but I am coughing and I stay away as much as I can for the sake of all those germs, and the vulnerability seeping into my mother's veins.

How did I get stuck in a life so physical and messy?

I am an adult, but not many days hence I was a child, absorbing the prevailing knowledge of the time that the spiritual is what matters and the body is what will decay. Let us leave this old world to burn. Into the childlike boxes of my mind, eager to learn, opening, shutting, is tucked the knowledge that the body is always what drags us down—the desire, the sin, the weakness, the need, the distraction, the falsity. The more holy a person becomes, the more the spirit triumphs. One can see victory in the denials, in the sleepless nights of prayer, the lengthy fasts, the celibacy.

I am only a child, and in the middle of my happy barefoot life I resolve to become pure spirit when I can. In between smelling new poplar leaves and digging in the sandbox, I evangelize the neighborhood and sculpt a life plan that involves unreached Africa and battle with demonic forces and many, many souls won to the Lord. I meet an adult who admits she too wanted to be a missionary in Africa, but well, life took her in a different direction. She is now a Minnesotan mother, her hands deep in soapy dishwater, telling me this. My six-year-old heart stands pitying, aloft, consecrated. I am not going to settle until I reach the pinnacle.

I am a child and then I am an adult, a destiny I stumbled to by the usual paths, a jumble of aspiration and default choices and birthdays. Finding myself in my thirties, a housewife immersed in childcare, is a detour on my life map for sure. I am not getting anywhere. I am on a treadmill of endless repeatable physical tasks producing what will be scarfed or soiled within moments. We are one hundred percent body: the graham cracker crumbs, the strands of loose hair, the jeans in a neat row on the clothesline, shredding our fingers and breaking our hearts on so much that will not last. Where is the victory, oh Lord, the kingdom, the power, the glory?

I am in my thirties before my early beliefs catch up with me and pull the meaning out of the world and find their names, like romanticism. And gnosticism, the worldview that I call A Neat Little Split Between Spirit and Body, for short. Rejecting the earth as divinely created, because it is too ugly, denying Jesus' full humanity, because he is too holy, and despairing of our time on this earth, because we are trapped in matter. All that is worthwhile is unseen, while the bodily things must be handled from the greatest possible distance (three layers of kid gloves, at least) lest they ensnare our hearts, choke our time, and corrupt our desires.

How much of my depression grows from this heretical root? From my desire for spiritual grandeur, my inability to see the sacred in the mundane? My inability to bring my body to Christ?

And who says spirit is pure? A good three-quarters of my sins hail from thence, by my calculations.

Where is our holy Jesus in the flesh if the flesh is tainted? Where is he when I am crying into my sleeve (made from cotton plants) while sitting on my couch (framed by wood from actual trees) because my precious little poppet (made of skin and blood and bones and a few other breathing things) has spit a hearty portion of milk (from a cow) onto my journal (paper and ink and heartbreak)?

I cough and cannot breathe.

I rock a baby who is not mine. She is sweet and sassy and sick. If she is not throwing up, she's asthmatic or feverish or runny-nosed. She is screaming in outrage because she's not accustomed to falling asleep this way and she doesn't care who knows it. I try laying her down. I try her tummy and her back, I try singing and silence, I try my presence and her solitude, I try swaddled and not swaddled, but she shrieks in panic that it is not right, this is not the way, something important is missing.

Her birth family is panicked as well, plaguing me with communication and dramatically manipulative requests. *Please please. I'm begging you. I know I'm late but I'm almost to the visit, please wait please.* A wide collection of kin waits to claim her, fights over who should be first in line and where she must not go, because this family member is not speaking to that one.

I pray for grace to outlast this assignment. I love this baby, she has accepted me as her caregiver, and I do not want to request the removal of any child from my home. But I do not know what to do, relationally or theologically or effectively. I feel my way with my body, resting and humming and rocking, wiping noses, getting out of bed multiple times a night and every morning anew, crouching in my pantry licking sustenance from a spoonful of peanut butter and honey.

My son pokes in his head, looking for me. I shove the spoon hastily into my mouth, out of sight. Not the whole spoon, I mean, just the dripping, nourishing, delectable end of it, and it floods my senses. *Son,* I say as firmly as I can through such a mouthful, *I am gathering shthrength to care for my children. Now go play.*

My ideology and identity may be tattered, but my physicality becomes a bedrock. Something firm to rest on, and push from there.

A friend of mine owns the only piece of clothing in the world that I covet, a lush, webbed scarf knitted in what she calls a dragon's wing pattern. Her mother has made it for her—not the kind of thing I can go out and buy. The softness of deep turquoise yarn is spattered with flecks of all colors. When she wraps it around her shoulders, she looks like a princess. Rich. Honored. Shielded. Even my children sense it, and their eyes fill with awe. My mother is ill, and my heart is filled with need. Who will take care of us? Under whose wing will I find shelter?

One day I receive a surprise package from another friend who lives hours away. Curious, I unwrap the paper and unfold a beautiful light turquoise scarf with sparkles of color all through. *Hey,* my children say, *that looks kind of like the dragon's wing.* Then I laugh in delight, and wrap it around me for the feeling of being covered, watched, protected. It is purchased, but it was purchased for me. I am now the kind of person someone would prepare a safeguard for.

I debated and debated about the color, my friend says. *I thought you liked blue.*

I love that scarf. I wear it in season and out of season, matching and not matching. *Hide me in the shadow of your wings* (Psalm 17:8). I wear it on the nights my husband is out and on the nights I sit up with the baby, and I wrap it around everyone I rock to sleep. When it is on my shoulders, I can feel his provision. Not a sparrow's wing, the somewhat shoddy defense I have always imagined in reading the Psalms, but something akin to a dragon's wing—the wide folds and glistening armor and unmatched power. I feel his hand over me, and I see him. He is huge and present and capable and beautiful, our source of nourishment, adequacy, and healing.

Still I cough and try to breathe.

One night, my foster baby quiets earlier than usual, on a night when I lay her in her crib in my bedroom in desperation, and let her cry while I put my head against a wall and inhale and exhale. When I peek in, she is lying on her back with her face entirely covered by her blanket, only her crown with its black fuzz of hair visible. She has pulled it up by herself and found her shelter. She has gone peacefully to sleep.

Voilà. She wants her face covered!

Not for the last time, I wish there were some way to have known. I study my new children like the Gospels, but it takes time to understand the code. I learn slowly, as I listen and as I do it wrong.

But I am not fond of blankets over tiny heads. For the next sleep, I lay a light mesh of sparkling turquoise over my baby's face. My scarf. As she relaxes, her eyelids drooping, I see her tucked beneath the wing of the Father.

> He who dwells in the shelter of the Most High
> will abide in the shadow of the Almighty . . .
> He will cover you with his pinions,
> and under his wings you will find refuge;
> his faithfulness is a shield and buckler. (Psalm 91:1, 4)

> Father of the fatherless and protector of widows
> is God in his holy habitation. (Psalm 68:5)

When the baby does not need the scarf, I sleep wrapped in it myself. Here is a curious thing, that the fabric can be as comforting to me as to her. I wear it at breakfast and to church and with my winter coat. I wear it until I can feel it around me whether I am wearing it or not.

In the shadow of your wings I will take refuge,
    till the storms of destruction pass by. (Psalm 57:1)

I wake at night fighting to take a breath, draped in a scarf that is not healing me, my room vacuum-packed and all the air gone. I find time and energy to visit the doctor, who tells me I am bronchospasming and gives me medicine. My bronchial passages are clapping together when I cough, and failing to release. That explains the desperate inhales, long and painful and audible, the struggle back to life.

How often would I have gathered your children together as
a hen gathers her brood under her wings, and you were not
willing! (Matthew 23:37)

I wear my scarf on a Thursday when I kiss my foster baby goodbye after three weeks of care, and pack her bags to move her to Grandma's house. I wear it two days later when my husband presents himself at the emergency department with the sharp pain of pneumonia. His chest has a knife in it and he's been trying not to disturb it, trying not to breathe deep. This coping strategy has not been kind to him.

He wraps himself in a blanket and spends the weekend laid out in our living room, done in.

I lick peanut butter when I need to, and cough, and sleep through the night at last, and take in air.

The phone rings on Monday.

It is our foster agency. The baby we just gave up is shuttling back into care. Her grandparents cannot handle the extended family pressure and conflict, the manipulating. She needs a home again—for now. She will move to another kinship home as soon as possible. Will we take her back?

We have learned how to say no, though it does not get easier with time, as you might think. It tears at the heart and cuts stripes with that knife in there and forces the oxygen from your body.

No, we cannot. We are so sick and we cannot heal, I'm sorry.

I lie prone on my bedroom floor beneath turquoise netting and pray with my posture. I am undone I am in need I have fallen down. Lord, I have nothing. Cover me.

When I touch this world, I can see that I am here. In it. I am grounded and I can see that Christ too is here. In it. With me. The unseen held in the seen, the seen held by the unseen.

What is omnipresence but divine pervasion of our finitude?

What is prayer but the offering of ourselves to the Almighty? What is prayer but spirit held with body, an angel in flesh gripped in a desperate fist? *I will not let you go until you bless me.* What is prayer but letting go at last? Feeling the holy slip from the grasp, and suddenly sensing its presence in the world all around? What is prayer but walking with a limp across the wet river and into the sunrise?

For the first time, I give myself permission to put my grief and longing into what I can touch. I have practiced this for years without understanding. I see it now. When I lost the hope of three babies in as many months, I know why I made three tiny blankets a few inches square, and why I held them against my cheek at night and saturated them with yearning. I know why I chose three poppy seeds and buried them in the soil.

I know why I cannot taste the Lord's Supper without being undone, the bread full-flavored in my mouth, the juice satisfying. Spirit in my hand, presence between my lips and teeth.

I know why green leaves above my head against blue sky became to me the arms of the Father, and why the wind in the treetops was the roaring of a Lion.

I know why I needed a white chocolate mocha on my breaktimes early in mothering. I know why the first sip of sweet foam in the silence brought tears to my eyes, immersed me unexpectedly in worship.

I know why I needed a succulent start from my grandma's garden to transplant into mine when she died, and why I bought a balloon to release when my grandpa followed her two months later.

I know why as a child, while I longed to become spirit with the Father, my body rejoiced in the grass under my stained feet, the wind and the tulips, the cherry seeds and the good earth. He was there, beyond my understanding, recognized by my heart. Inside my joy and my body. Inside his world.

Tie me to yourself. Wrap me close to your presence.

Tangibility reaches backward and forward in my life. I pray with my body. I pray with my hands holding to his skirt. I pray with a scarf and I pray with a candle. I call it an Everything Is Going to Be All Right candle, a plain taper in a sheath of tinfoil on my kitchen counter. When it burns out, I find another to replace it. It is a prayer, a confession, a mustard seed. My striking of the match is my placing of trust, my holding to truth.

You are with me.

I worship with my fingers on the piano keys, with my tears of salt. I learn to get more of my body involved when I come to him in the secret corners of my life—I stand, I lift my hands to him, I lie prostrate, I kneel. I close my eyes when, unexpectedly, I notice him. I ask for more. Small things, like strength to open jars and peace to hold my tongue. His presence at our table, with my homemade pizza.

Save me, Lord, from the unbelief that makes me blind to the Here of Emmanuel.

The magic of him entering our world is not so we can leave it to enter his. It is the magic of encountering him at every turn, here and now, then and later; no place on earth so ugly that he will not grace it. He is where the sunlight falls and where the darkness coils, where children run in lighthearted hope and where they are victimized and laid low. He is praised by the birds, saluted by the trees. He is in the wind. He is the great infiltrator, and his creation knows it, groans for his full coming, as do we. We watch not for liberation, all spirit set free of this old world to soar, but the opposite: spirit pushing into body, into the created earth brimful of his redemption. Every space sacred. All the creatures made what they were meant to be.

> For the creation was subjected to futility, not willingly, but because of him who subjected it, in hope that the creation itself will be set free from its bondage to corruption and obtain the freedom of the glory of the children of God. (Romans 8:20-21)

He is over the cookie crumbs and under the cobwebs. He is wrapped in the branches of the hemlocks in my woods. He is between my floorboards, inside my walls, all over my roof. There is no place my feet can rest where he is not. He crafts the eggs for my breakfast, brings the water for our baths, draws near in the silence of our sleeping. He sits with me in our unfinished house without shame, invented the body fluids that cleanse us and do not contaminate, sees the holes in our socks before I do and does not flinch away.

He is here. The depth of my inadequacy and need is matched only by the depth of his presence and sufficiency. I am a creature, in need of mercy. He gives me permission to be human, a being who has unwanted hair and unwelcome tears and unfinished business. Created this way by his deliberate design. We are body and spirit together, he and I, and he in all.

And so I cook spaghetti noodles. I swallow prescribed cap-sules of healing, and my cough lightens, loosens. I wipe the last runny nose, for now. I change another diaper and give thanks. I lose my temper. I hand a spoon of peanut butter to my child. I tie small shoes, the cotton laces supple and slipping through my fingers. I lay my hand on the bare skin that is now my mother's head, and sense the new-grown fluff of hair that soon will soften it. I recycle empty medicine bottles. I tend my houseplants and squish a spider. I breathe without pain, and I rejoice.

10

LOOKING INSIDE

When you consider your own life . . .

1. What tangible objects or practices signal Jesus' presence to you?

2. Do you deal with fear that his world will distract you from him? (It is a valid concern.) How do you avert that danger?

3. What helps you see purpose in the physical world—his divine presence in the mundane?

4. How do you worship?

Keeping a running list of things you are thankful for has become a common practice, and it is an excellent one. A twist I recommend is writing only sensory or tangible things on the list for a time, as a way to open your eyes to Jesus' goodness and reality on this earth.

11

Victory of Another Kind

The Release of Refusing to Fight

PRELUDE
TO THE FORGOTTEN ONE

I am the light you cannot see, searching, piercing—not the mild sunlight of a summer day or the glimmer of candle and firelight, but the inescapable blaze of a streetlight on a deserted parking lot when all around is darkness.

I love you.

I saw the look on your face when it happened again, the thing you feared. It was only there for a second before you hid it, but I saw. You were not alone.

When you look around, you see the smiling Others whose lives seem to work—their bodies, their faces, their families.

They seem to skip over the hard bits, or laugh them off, or overcome them. They seem so on top of things, and in the darkness you wonder why you are the odd one out.

I know the grief you carry, the tightening of your heart when the subject comes up, the dread of insensitive questions and curious glances. I know how you cry when people move in to care, and cry when they do not.

I know you worry that it will be too much for you, that this thing will make you crack if you face it, that the price is too high. I know exhaustion. I see it in your eyes. I know what you have sacrificed, and though you wonder, I am the one who knows it is not in vain. It will never be in vain.

I see you.

I know you.

You are not the only one.

I know the things you hold close to the chest, the horrors you cannot share lest your world cave in around you. In scores of stripes across my bleeding back I carried them for you. I carry you still.

In your loneliness I am there. When the night closes in, you are held in my light. When everyone else has someone, when the silence of the people who matter the most screams at you, when you've forgotten how to be the person you were, when the radiant ship sails without you, I am there.

I know what lies beneath your frustration and your turmoil, I know the palpable midnight of your fear. I am there when it yawns beneath you, when frantically you flail your way to solid ground, panting, shrieking.

Darling, you could fall all the way down and I would be *there*.

You are mine.

—Jesus

The world is so full of fine books and sweet kids and good love that it's enough to go on, enough to live for. But there were many times I wondered; and in my heart I wonder still.

We host a range of children, from infant to school age, from blue-eyed to bronzed. I love them all—love the shy ones and the rowdy, love the silly and the earnest, love the delayed and the precocious. I love the silken blond pigtails and the dimpled brown cheeks. I have dreamed of a brown-skinned child of my own, even when I did not approve of my dreaming. (Between *do not covet* and *do not commit adultery,* my options are somewhat limited.)

Did you know that sometimes the Lord Jesus gives you the desire for what is coming before it comes?

Since our earliest days of fostering, filling out those papers and checking every box on the color list for children we are willing to consider, my heart holds a picture that grows clearer by the month: a little boy and little girl of color. They are eighteen months apart and she is oldest. They are beautiful.

It's not uncommon for me to receive intuitions that I attribute to God, though I have often been mistaken in my rendering. The ones that do not go away are the ones I pay attention to. Always I hold with an open hand and wait to see, but sometimes in them I recognize his voice and fingerprint, his promise.

I grow these two babies in my heart, not knowing if they are real, or if they will ever come to me. For me to mother them, something would have to go terribly wrong in their world. This I do not wish for them.

On official papers, we state ourselves willing to receive only one foster child this time, because of our inadequacy with the twins. In my head, I agree with the wisdom of this decision, but in my heart, I treasure the foolishness of hope for what is coming, before it comes.

It is a long time coming. We are without a foster placement for a year, growing and breathing, working on our house, working with our children. We recover strength and laughter and optimism. In the winter of our fifteenth year of marriage, we get a call on a Saturday afternoon. Two children need to be moved immediately from another foster care arrangement. They have been in the system the better part of a year, and kinship options have been ruled out. Our agent is apologetic. *I know you said one. We just need help for the weekend, until we can find them a pre-adoptive home next week. Everyone is out of the office, and I'm in the airport at the moment, leaving town. Can you go pick them up?*

The baby is a year and a half. His sister is turning three.

My husband and I always make these decisions together, although the one who is not on the phone does not always get the full scoop. Listening in on his conversation, I say yes because I want two kids and I think this is a long-term placement. I can't believe he's saying yes. He says yes because he knows it is two kids, but only for the weekend, and we are not locking ourselves into something we may not be able to handle.

These children need the yes we are longing to say again. Perhaps for our part we need redemption. We need to pour love on two little people and have it be enough, have us be enough. Maybe that is a selfish need. I think it probably is. I can feel the tension in my forehead, and the fear in my heart when he says it's for the weekend. *I don't think I can give up any more kids,* I say. *If it goes well, is there any reason we can't be their pre-adoptive home?*

I don't think there is, love. We'll see.

After all of that, he tells me the children are biracial, and I begin to cry. The picture in my heart comes into focus, and I know this is a yes that we are meant to say.

An hour later, the children I have already seen and loved in my spirit enter into my physical house. I know them. There they are, in skin. The girl-child's mouth is exquisite—plump and full and adorable. There are tears in her eyes from the stress of leaving yet another home. The boy-child turns on a megawatt grin, and my heart reaches out its arms and takes these children in.

Every foster parent knows this truth. As hard as you try to love all children, and as greatly as you succeed, a few wiggle their way into your love further and faster than you could have imagined. It is a love that goes beyond silly wishes, genetics, and happenstance. This child. This parent. We recognize each other, and whatever happens later on, we will never again be separate, never free of this connection. *My son. My daughter.*

Once again, we are fully engrossed in childcare. Our two newcomers fit exactly around our baby, one older and one younger. We are raising triplets, lining up the cups of milk, the bath times, and the church clothes. On good days, we are an endearing little entourage. On bad days, small fingers push pebbles through the grill of our van, bathroom accidents are orchestrated deliberately and in protest, toys become sophisticated weaponry, long strips of paint are pulled from bedroom walls, and toilets are splashed in joyfully when Mother Is Not Looking.

Life is not easy. But however hard it is, we now know what is harder: saying goodbye. We will not go through that again if we can help it. Every few months, we are asked if we are still on track to adopt if needed; all the signs are pointing that way. We never waver on the decision we make that first weekend. Our losses and big no have prepped us for this full bonding and big yes. We are stronger than we were. More committed. More supported. Our children are two years older, our older three excellent siblings and playmates to the younger three. We are all in.

Better yet, the children take their places in our family. They have experienced love, and know how to give it and take it. They form firm bonds with us and our kiddos, call us Mommy and Daddy. We have margin to hold all six. We spend hours snuggling our new ones, merging identities, learning how to do it their way, chattering, playing outside. We fall in love with who they are.

For a year, they are ours.

The birth parents, both of them talented and likable people, are failing prodigally, taking no steps toward the healing that would permit their children to return home. And for the first time in our fostering experience, we are unable to form a relational connection with the biological family. We try to work for their good, honor their preferences, ask their advice, but we are shut out, fully rejected before we are partly known. We thought we knew how to do relationships across this divide. Maybe we are just the wrong people. Too treacherous. Too much in the lead in this race.

We keep trying, wishing we knew what we were doing wrong.

In the fall, we receive the date for a weighty hearing, an involuntary termination of parental rights. At this point, it is an open-and-closed case. I wish I could say that we grieve for their losses. I think we do, I know we try. But we have seen so much destruction this past year that we long for them to be past the repeated pain. We make plans to honor their parents, to keep the good parts of the legacy always in the children's minds. By Christmas, we will be their only family. Next year—adoption.

A second rending appears on our horizon. Our second son, who has walked a long and difficult and funny and outrageous and passionate journey from age one to age eleven (and survived by the mercy of Jesus) is nosediving. We are very, very worried about him. We research, we hug, we take time to talk. We match him with a therapist and find a behavior specialist consultant. He has friends. He likes his siblings, both birth and foster (all but one, who was born here and hence rather permanent). He is a gifted and intelligent young man. But his unhappiness, anger, and aggression is eating him up. *What can we do for him? Please tell us.* We don't need him to be someone different. We need him to be what he is, what we know Jesus made him.

We arrange a psychiatric evaluation, in hopes of getting medication. We drive him to appointments. We sing bellowing duets with him out the open windows of our vehicle. We respond with anger when we should respond with firm authority, or grace. We confess this to him. We share his favorite snacks. We forgive. We pray. We hope.

We use every tool we know, and we fight as hard as we can to keep our son on track, to help him win his battle. But we go from bad to worse. He has no internal checks on his behavior and needs continual, focused supervision. We work with the same issues at age eleven that we did at age two—rage, deceit, theft, impulsivity, tantrums—but they have darkened and intensified. When he's angry, he is prone to episodes of violence that frighten even him. He comes to me afterward shaking and crying. One terrifying afternoon, he goes missing from school.

We cannot go on as we are. What we can scarcely manage at age eleven will be impossible at age fifteen. We cannot ensure that he and the people around him are safe. We must get help.

We find a therapeutic wilderness boys camp with a long-term intervention program, and we begin to buy supplies. A rain poncho and water shoes. Flannel shirts. Winter socks. Sandals. We have had this option in the back of our minds for a long time, pushed firmly into the background, squashed down. Will it hurt or help him? How will he live without us, we without him? I have always known we could not bear it, but here I am buying towels and washcloths online, long thermal underwear, two pairs of hiking boots.

Jesus. Give me strength to bring my son back to the light.

January is the selected month: the bitterest time to deliver a child to the boondocks, to shelters made out of skinned trees and tarps. Another boy is graduating, and there is a vacancy in the camp on the mountain.

The camp will not accept boys against their will, and in the end my son is the one who chooses to go.

In December, only days before our foster children's hearing for the termination of parental rights, we receive another phone call, a game changer. *Since we filed the paperwork to terminate, their birth mother has begun doing everything right. We need to reschedule court for a couple of months later and give her time to prove herself.*

I cry for three days, feeling cold sick terror. I attend a family team meeting, where I sit beside the biological mom with my hands strangling each other in my lap, and hold as still as I can, and say the kindest things I can think of while we go around the table and tell all the good progress she is making. *Great job! Wow, you are really doing this! I think at this rate, you have every reason to expect your children back with you soon!*

Oh my Lord, these kids are mine. I will fight anything and anyone for them.

They are mine like they are born to me. But they are not. I have treasured them for years, long before I knew them. I have washed their faces and fixed their bruises and made them eat green beans. I have received the screaming and the sweet kisses and the sticky fingers and the clover bouquets. I have witnessed their first prayers, heard the name of Jesus on its maiden voyage across their lips. I have been given every certainty that they are bone of my bones and heart of my heart, and that a legal order will make them free to be adopted. I have promised my soul to them as Mother. Do not take them from me. What will be left?

But they are not mine, and this story is not about me. The best-case scenario is always the first family, not the second. You might say the foster parents are innocent bystanders, pulled into dramas in which we do not feature. Our job is to love and facilitate and help as long as we are needed, and not to steal the show. We are stagehands setting up the actors for success and joy, helping them look good, and dimming the lights for the happy ending.

(Then slipping away during the standing ovation for hysterics and a stiff gin in the cold alley outside.)

That is our job. To return to sender whenever possible. To nurture faith when faith does not seem warranted. To remember that *mine* and *not mine* can live side by side in a human heart.

What kind of a person would I be if I fought for these children? When their mother, so inadequate, so hopeless all these months, is taking her stand as a sufficient parent? When she needs our belief in her, a friend to babysit once a month, an extended network of support? Who am I to kick the props out from under an emerging family?

I feel a divine hand on my mouth, shushing my sass, holding my tongue. There is a palpable warning in the air: *Do not mess up what is happening, girl. Lay it down. Let it go.*

But he gave me the longing, the intuition of what was to come. He gave me a year of assurances that they are meant to be with us. It's like Christmas morning and a beautiful child opens her present to find the bicycle she has always wanted, the basket, the streamers, the pretty pink seat, spokes twinkling with jewels. Her father sits there watching her eyes sparkle, letting her run her hands over its perfection, and then he says, *That's not actually for you,* and he picks it up and gives it to her sister.

Who does that to their child?

I know you can't give your whole heart as a foster parent and survive. I was tricked into it by the inexplicably fiendish move of an all-seeing God. I wait for him to explain himself, to turn this situation around, or to laugh and say, *Just kidding. I got mixed up and gave you the wrong vision.* What is he doing? He would not possibly have given this perfect gift to me only to take it away again on purpose.

Would he?

I spend a lot of time biting my lips. My chest hurts.

I do not believe this family can succeed. I've seen too much. I drive to visits praying that I can smile, that I can speak kindness, that I can be bland and sweet and good-hearted. I fight the inky seepage of hatred, but it stains my best moments.

At any moment, she could fail, but instead she stands stronger. She grows secure and faithful (to them). She is cool and silent and winning (to me). Of course she should win, if that is a possibility, but in my mind, she doesn't play fair. I tell myself that if it were a clean fight, I could win. But it feels to me like one of us has access to every loophole in the book, to an entire system of people eager to enable her and stack the cards her way, and the other has her hands tied behind her back. (Someday, I will know this is exactly as it should be. I do not know it now.) I am losing in a big way, and I go on losing.

I lose what I have built with them, as more and more of themselves finds its way to a new home, and their behaviors wear thin in the transition. I lose our present, the moments growing shorter and more fraught. I lose our future, all the pieces I wanted to share with them, all the birthdays that were coming, every hug ahead of us, the first day of first grade, sports and music and long talks, teenage crushes, careers, wedding days, my grandchildren. I lose it, one day at a time.

One day we are given the court date for the children's return home. Another day we get the intense visit schedule until then, and see how little they will be ours. *I can fight this,* I think. *I can ask for my rights, I can require courtesy, I can get back my own. THIS IS NOT FAIR.*

And then I hear his words in my mind. *But I say unto you, that ye resist not evil: but whosoever shall smite thee on thy right cheek, turn to him the other also. And if any man will sue thee at the law, and take away thy coat, let him have thy cloak also* (Matthew 5:39-40 KJV).

In this new Jesus-kingdom scene, it looks like the greedy-grabby fighting meanie-pants people win. And we let them.

How, Lord, how?

I kneel by my bed and cry. I can feel a physical lump in my throat from how much this way hurts, how hard it is to choose, and how much I hate my enemies, the family whose hopes and interests are in direct conflict with my own, and who won't play nice to get there.

So I keep making all the visits on time, and I help the children buy their mother a special gift for Christmas. Maybe I bake something to share. Maybe I think about putting poison in it.

I can do all the right things, I tell the Divine Silence. *I can be an adult and work for her good and be pleasant-if-bumbling and say words that I mean but do not feel. I can shield her from my grief. I can help her increase into the mommy role, in a dozen trivial ways, while I decrease. I can even praise my enemy's progress (it is real progress), warmly to her and faithfully behind her back to those who need to know. Thank you for this grace.*

But, oh Lord, please. When you look into my soul and see the heartbreak and the fury, I beg that you do not see a hypocrite and a liar. I am choked by my own interests. Hiding beneath my good deeds is a desperate desire for her to crash and burn. Deep inside I am seeking only my own, and I cannot purge it away. Look on me, Lord.

When I rise from my knees, I do not feel peace. I feel wrenched out and wrung tight. I feel beset with doubts, crusty with drying tears. I feel touchy and irritable with small demands.

If God is going to save us, I need him to do it soon. I need him to tip his hand. I want him to be on my side, to be the nice God I believed in who does not let his kids face devastation in efforts of obedience to him. If he's not going to show up with a sword, he should at least be showing up with a magical elixir of comfort, hope, peace. Where is he?

I become unable to speak to him unless I am on a treadmill. I mean a real treadmill. I cannot meet with him unless I am running up against the barriers of what my body can handle. I run until my muscles burn and my lungs sharpen, and because I am holding on to the handles I can keep my eyes closed and I can feel him there, just beyond my face, outside my lips, so present and so still while my world whirls and my body sweats. I whisper to him my hatred, my doubt, my destruction.

He does not permit me to pray against her, and it feels like death to pray for her success, but that is what I do. I pray, *If she can pull this off and be a good mother, bless everything she is doing and make her strong.* And I cannot help but add, *And if she cannot, please let it crumble soon.*

She grows stronger.

He does not explain himself.

In this place I am nothing but dependent on him, and I cannot bear it. I fill my days. I pack the last bags, gather precious possessions from all over the house, buy warm extra outfits so they have a good stash to move with and she doesn't have to buy clothes first thing. On the last morning, I drive them to her house and I drop them off and my eyes do not cry and I thank her for letting us love them. I give her everything and she looks at me, silent, and I hug the kids and say a cheerful goodbye.

I step back into my van and I will never be the same.

There is a cold square of ice in my chest, and God is not good, and I need him to be what he is not. I need, I need, and he is there but not there. I have never heard my husband weep as he does now, and I sob against his chest, and our baby wails her heartbreak for the leaving until she falls into exhausted sleep.

A scattering of January snow ices the ground on the day we drive up the mountain with our second son. Camp is no longer a possibility, but an imminent reality. There are three people in this vehicle, and only two will be riding back down. I wait for my child to say, *Here is the fire and the wood, but where is a lamb for the sacrifice?*

But he is quiet, a little pale, very focused. I beg God to let him live.

We leave him there on the altar.

Three children in six weeks.

Of the three that are left, two are in school, and one is a very gentle and obedient preschooler. My house is so silent I can hear the carpet compressing and releasing after my daughter's footsteps. Smush shsh smush shsh.

If there is anything I have learned in the past fifteen years—this is what all survivors say, to convince themselves their struggles are worth it at some cosmic level—if there is anything I have learned, it is that the act of loving people you cannot save can take the legs right out from under you. Some call it compassion fatigue. Some call it vicarious trauma. I call it crucifixion.

I hang between the Father who will not speak to me and the world whose brokenness is unending torture. *Why have you forsaken me?* I have trusted God and walked his path and it is killing me and he has let me down. Worse still, I watch my children hang with nails in their wrists and I cannot end it for them. I have put away my sword at his command, so help me, and the legion of angels did not descend.

THE REASON I AM SO ANGRY IS THAT I AM GIVING EVERY-THING TO HEAL US AND IT IS NOT WORKING. I'M TIRED OF BREAKING MYSELF OPEN AGAINST A WORLD THAT REFUSES TO CHANGE. I AM ANGRY THAT GOD, WHO IS SUPPOSED TO BE MAK-ING THINGS RIGHT, ISN'T EVEN HELPING ME DO WHAT I CAN.

I have lived through loss and I am here to tell you that God may be the Savior, but sometimes he hangs bleeding too and you do not have deliverance. Sometimes you die waiting for him to act. That is what happened to Jesus when he screamed *My God, my God* and the slow moments slipped by him, each one a whipping, and he was naked and pierced and dripping and thirsty while the holy men of his day circled him, sneering, *He trusted in God; let him deliver him now if he will have him* (Matthew 27:43 NKJV), until the last of the oxygen left his body. Jesus was heard. But he died slowly and God was there and God did not save him. God forsook him to his death. The Greek word in Romans is *paredoken*, elsewhere translated *betrayed. He that spared not his own Son, but* DELIVERED HIM UP *for us all, how shall he not with him also freely give us all things?* (Romans 8:32 KJV).

This is what it means to be a Jesus follower when they're taking you down. To hold on to faith with hands that can't grip, because they have nails in them. To dangle between your heaven and your hell. Not to act, but to suffer being acted upon—to permit the happenings to be enacted in your story and on your body. To love and to wait and to lose.

I don't want any part of it. I would run if I could, but it is too late.

Perhaps you think I am overinflating myself, comparing my suffering to his. You are right. He suffers in incomparable supremacy and purity as the Lamb of God, not only in his passion but in all the years since the dawn of time, as his creatures strike his face and crush the thorns of their curse onto one another's heads. I am not him. The truth is that my own inadequacies and sins weight my body, bring it down, suck the oxygen out of the sky.

But you are also wrong. When we engage with his love in a world of injustice and hatred, when we hang for our trust in the sovereignty and goodness of the Father, when the pain that should have landed on a culprit lands on a willing surrogate, our suffering is *of the same type* as his, as the raindrop is of the same water as the ocean. Though the one is insignificant and easily lost in the other, thousands of its kind make up the whole and carry it from place to place all over the world, raining down upon the earth the fractured gentleness, multifaceted goodness, and human empathy of Christ. When we lay down the need to fight for ourselves—our persons, our interests, and the people we love—we open the door for redemption on a scale too vast and eternal for words. And it feels a lot like dying.

Love is the only thing that redeems, and love cannot live in this world without being wrenched on a rack.

I sit with a counselor one day and from my pain come words I didn't know were in me. *I have believed in him all my life,* I say. *And I know how silly it is to give up on him when things don't work out for me. But I have no idea what he's doing.* With the words come a fury I cannot quantify, like my words are the spit on his beard and the stripes on his back.

My counselor speaks softly. *No one on a cross remembers the plan. You are caught up between heaven and earth—what will be, and what is.*

There is only one thing to do on a cross, he says.

Die.

My son, my son far from home. I love my camping boy and I miss him and I cannot protect him and I cannot save him. If this doesn't work, I don't have a backup plan.

And I am not the mother of my two. When I reach for them in my mind they are gone, like a tooth, like a limb. I can love others and I can be a mom again but I do not get them back, they are irreplaceable and gone and they are not mine.

What does the Father think when he looks at his children?

I too have turned my son over to hard things, and I too have let him cry into his pillow, and sometimes I cannot live with myself for that. But all the while I talk to him and I say, *Only a little longer* and *I love you* and *You are precious to me* and *I am always here* and *What a good job you are doing* and *My son.*

What can you say to a Father when you don't have a word and you don't hear a word and the anguish is ice and blood in your heart?

Die.

It is the only way.

For months, it will hurt so much that I lie in bed in the morning leaking tears into my hands, knowing I can't get up. And then, I do. My two stockinged feet on the floor are the bravest things I've ever done. There is a new day, and a fried egg for breakfast, and another child to hold.

In time, I do come to see this. On Christmas morning, I am not the child who opens the bike. I am the sister across the room, to whom it is loaned. He fully intends to return his gifts to the child to whom he gave them, as often and as soon as he can. This is the heart of the Father, the heart of the suffering Jesus, and the greatest success. I got confused about who I was.

Confusion is a necessary part of deepening trust, and I believe in doubt. For me, it has become a sacred birthplace of faith.

My jubilant sister will not fall. He will uphold her and knit her family back together. As she becomes secure in her motherhood, she will not have to flail and scratch to claim her own. She will begin to trust our friendship, as we see her winning and only increase our support. We will not be cut out of her children's lives, as I feared. She will grant us a place in their ongoing story, arrange times for them to come over and play, and keep us updated. She will invite us to birthday parties, and take us out to eat on Mother's Day. She will let us see into her strong, beautiful personhood, her fears, her successes, her humor. She will become an excellent mother, and a friend.

The Christ who did not allow me to fight is crafting a beautiful work. He will call this family, and oh miracle of grace! She will step toward him.

I am permitted to see this too. Hallelujah.

11

LOOKING INSIDE

Scripture has a lot to say about suffering with Christ, in Christ, and as Christ. Listen for just a moment.

> For he has not despised or abhorred the affliction of the afflicted, and he has not hidden his face from him, but has heard, when he cried to him. (Psalm 22:24)

> Now I rejoice in my sufferings for your sake, and in my flesh I am filling up what is lacking in Christ's afflictions for the sake of his body, that is, the church. (Colossians 1:24)

> Now who is there to harm you if you are zealous for what is good? But even if you should suffer for righteousness' sake, you will be blessed. Have no fear of them, nor be troubled, but in your hearts honor Christ the Lord as holy . . . For it is better to suffer for doing good, if that should be God's will, than for doing evil. For Christ also suffered once for sins, the righteous for the unrighteous, that he might bring us to God, being put to death in the flesh but made alive in the spirit. (1 Peter 3:13-18)

> Beloved, do not be surprised at the fiery trial when it comes upon you to test you, as though something strange were happening to you. But rejoice insofar as you share Christ's sufferings, that you may also rejoice and be glad when his glory is revealed. Therefore let those who suffer according to God's will entrust their souls to a faithful Creator while doing good. (1 Peter 4:12-13, 19)

The Spirit himself bears witness with our spirit that we are children of God, and if children, then heirs—heirs of God and fellow heirs with Christ, provided we suffer with him in order that we may also be glorified with him. (Romans 8:16-17)

The saying is trustworthy, for: If we have died with him, we will also live with him; if we endure, we will also reign with him; if we deny him, he also will deny us; if we are faithless, he remains faithful—for he cannot deny himself. (2 Timothy 2:11-13)

Where have you experienced this kind of suffering? What do you think about crucifixion?

12

In His Silence

The Miracle of Being Prayed For

I have never seen a nail pounded deep into a human body
The flesh torn and held by the metal
But I have seen
The flat and stapled wound on the chest of a friend
Where once a breast nurtured children.
Oh God, give me grace to look gently, and not to turn away.

I have never seen thorns pressed into a forehead,
Red drops snaking their way down a face gray with pain
But I have seen
The devastation on the face of a child

When the last tie to the familiar was snipped through—
But we cannot be separated. We promised Daddy we would
    stay together.
I have felt the hopeless sobs against my chest, seen
The light snuffed out of the eyes.
Oh God, give me grace to hold, and to heal.

I have never seen a man's back worn to shreds by a cruel whip
More raw, in the end, than whole
But I have seen
Slits in the wrists of a friend, crisscrossed lines of despair
As she walked away from rehab, picking at the scabs.
It was the last time I saw her alive.
Oh God, give me grace to know and be known
By hope.

I have never seen the last clothes stripped
Bartered, diced for
While the soldiers laughed and the Christ of the world hung
    dying
But I have seen
A child with nothing from his past but the outfit he was
    wearing
And memories fresh in his mind of uniforms, disintegra-
    tion, goodbyes.
I have watched him struggle to rest in a strange bed, to trust
    new people,
To get his untrained fingers around a belt buckle and a crayon
    and a table knife and a toothbrush
To find home again when all has been stolen.
Oh God, give me grace to reach out my arms
And commit my spirit.

I have never seen a man accursed by the world, forsaken by
   the Father

Hanging between earth and sky

But in word pictures, I have seen my own beloved son weep

In the silence of his tent at night when home is far away

And the devil says, *You are worthless. You are alone. You are
   such a bad one.*

I have seen a dying man in a hospital bed groping for words
   to say the last things.

I have looked far into eyes of a child trapped in genetic disability.

Where is he? How much does he know, in this lucid, connected moment?

I have seen love silent, forbidden, bloodshot.

I have seen my sister's and my mother's heads bereft of hair,
   their bodies made listless by chemo.

I have seen the anguish in the mug shot eyes of a mother, a
   woman at the end of everything.

I have seen the confusion of the elderly as the world wavers
   and shifts around them and they reach for one hand to
   hold, one set of eyes to lock on to, one unchanging point
   of reference.

I have heard in my small way the agony of the ages, the death
   cry of the heart

And beneath it, I hear the scream

Of the Man I never saw

But recognize

In the pain of his creatures:

The dying God, the pinioned Almighty.

Oh God, give me grace to follow in his steps.

Confession: There have been many events in my life that nearly took me under, but from this one I know I will not recover. I am tipping my head as far as I can to the sky, but when I gulp I taste salt in my mouth, my nose. I am going to drown.

I am part of a growing wave of women who are honest about what mothering is like underneath, the gritty cracker-crumbed floors and the yelling, the late-night food binges and the safety pins beneath the perfect Easter outfits. But I am not talking only about messiness, I am talking about wreckage, when the good choices don't deliver and the efforts fail and the pastor husband steps down from leadership to repent and heal and the children need what we cannot give them and God does not uphold our world-saving and every step toward good feels bought with blood.

Gradually, the pain centers in my chest. At first it is pneumonia and afterward it is not. It centers and congeals there, solidifies into a weight I carry and cannot get rid of.

They say there's simple grief and complex. Mine is not simple. When I see my former foster children, they are not mine and I let them go all over again. When my son comes home for a visit, I have five days to pour six weeks of affection on him before I drive him back up the same road and he is gone.

How to heal when the wound is always freshened?

Motions, motions, motions. There are so many motions and all of them must be gone through. I am fostering another child or two and I am doing well at bonding with them despite my fear that I cannot in my grief. I am. My heart is still open to let people in, but I am not talking to God much. I stop telling him what I feel and what I want. I am afraid he will use it against me and I am angry at him (and, inexplicably, at my husband) for getting me into these situations and then not protecting me. Isn't that their job?

If I'm not talking to God, I'm not hearing anything from him either. Only at church do I hear him, which I don't want to attend, because it is exposing and religious and vulnerable, and because I always cry. The songs are so beautiful, and in that place with the people of God all around me, their silver voices filling my heart, I can finally see him just a little bit. I can see that his face is kind.

On Monday, Tuesday, Wednesday, God is silent. On Thursday I have nothing to say to him. On Friday and Saturday he has probably forsaken me, and do I even belong to him? On Sunday I go to church against my will; it seems that going to church is something pastors' wives do. On Sunday I belong and I cry.

I do not sleep well. I dream too much: of the backs of people I love as they walk away from me, of crucial things forgotten, of impossible tasks I cannot complete.

By now, after walking through saying goodbye to children before, I expect the rough nights, the suddenly materializing insomnia, some anxiety. I expect the slumping. I go to bed late and I get up late and I make lunch late and I forget to plan dinner. I lose my train of thought. I don't want to go out in public. Inside me is utter silence, a stillness that engulfs the world.

Usually it is only music that breaks through the silence. Sometimes a hug. Sometimes a difficult scene in a book or a movie. Then there is screaming, the kind of crying that breaks the soul and feels like blood and nausea and the ripping of tendons, and I don't want that.

I am always surprised to find how irritable I am in grief. I am snappy with my children, unable to handle the little annoyances, like someone sneezing on my skin by mistake or my son forgetting to put a clean trash bag in the can. I am like a woman in labor, stretched so near the breaking point that the housefly nosing and buzzing around the hospital window is unbearable. While I am in the jaws of death here, even the flies are against me? Someone catch this one and beat him to a pulp and leave his thorax to rot on the windowsill.

All of this is familiar, if awful.

But why is this grief so physical?

It settles into my body, messing up my breathing, my hormones, my heart rhythms. My newfound cardiologist says, *It acts like AFib. Really? At your age, with zero risk factors?* I want to sleep all the time, and I drop things, and I am shaky and prone to headaches. The skin of my face will recover, but it ages noticeably, dry and porous.

I want to beg everyone I meet for an answer, a drug, a pill I can swallow to take the edge off it. *Please. I hurt. Please do something for me. Show me how to breathe.* But no one can say.

Who is God and what does he want me to do? Do I crawl into his lap like a child, or bend my back before his lash, or stand strong in truth against the onslaughts of the enemy? Each is beyond my power, and none feels right. I don't know. I cannot find how to come to him.

I have prayed for so many people in distress. *I'm praying for you* is arguably the most used sentence in Christianity, right next to *Let us rise for the benediction.* I've come to God on behalf of so many needs that supplication has at times crowded out worship, thanksgiving, and confession. Now when God and I are silent, others pray for me. I don't have the strength of faith to ask for it, but they offer.

I watch the different ways they come to him, the postures.

One friend talks to him like she is picking up the phone for a chat with a close friend. She is informal and immediate, picks up right where she left off. She laughs and stumbles for words and finds beautiful ones after several tries: understanding what she believes and needs as she talks about it, as is so often the case when verbalizing to a friend.

Another prays with power. I can see her standing erect before the throne of God, the hands of her spirit raised, her words blessings and curses and strength and beauty and authority in the heavens. I know that what she prays comes true.

One day I sit with a third, and when she prays for me, she starts way back at creation and the cross and I watch her approach the Lord through all the ways, slowly: through gratitude and praise and confession and emptiness, into the light. She arrives only gradually to the issues at hand, and I find my face wet.

My husband prays with his shoulders bowed and his hands on my head. He prays truth and healing. I feel his gentle protection, his advocacy, over me like a blanket. *This one is with me, Jesus. She does not know what to say to you, but we are here together. We come.*

For many months, this is how I survive. The people I love speak for me. I find I can talk to him when someone comes along. With.

I rediscover the Lord's Prayer, the ancient words of Christ translated into my language and my time. *Our Father. Deliver us from evil. Thy will be done in earth, as it is in heaven. Hallowed be thy name.*

My friend gives me a prayer book, and old English phrases fall from my lips into his ears. They aren't mine, but they become mine in the speaking when I can't think of what to say. They are true and good, and they orient my heart toward what is right. They pull me out of myself into the big plans of God, to my suffering fellow man, to the world in need of a Savior. They lay me low.

Late in the year, I come to the Lord's Supper at my church on a dark clear evening, and my longing for Jesus is palpable in my throat. By now I have lived through months of quiet between us. I am so hungry. I want that bit of bread as a newborn wants his mother's milk. I am starving.

I open my mouth and receive the bread, and as my teeth sink into it, I find I have received the Christ. He is standing there before me, inside me, visible to my spirit, and I clap my hand over my mouth and shake and my throat hurts from holding in the sobbing. I see him at last. He is there and I know my posture: my own posture: after all this time I know what he wants from me, and my whole person is giving it, unquestioning.

He wants me on my knees, my hands held out. He wants this word from me. *Anything.* Not the limp acquiescence of non-desiring, but the passion of needing and giving and surrendering and yearning all at the same time. To long without demanding. To surrender without discarding. To break without falling. Anything, my Lord. He wants me trusting when I don't know. He wants me worshiping.

This is my posture.

I take the hormone pills my doctor recommends for regulating my irrational body, and I undergo several heart tests and agree to my specialist's recommendation. Catheter ablation. It is not surgery, but it is anesthesia and sedation. With only the tiniest of entrance points, he will look into my heart and see where the bad rhythms are coming from, and burn tiny bits of my physical heart. The scar tissue growing there in the next couple of months will prevent further signals of irregularity and harm.

I find it ironic that scars can heal you.

We write dozens and dozens of letters to a boy in a camp on the mountain, and watch the mail anxiously for his words, which are frequent and penciled and honest. He passes through the honeymoon stage rapidly, unleashes all the behaviors and then some, fights hard, hits the wall of his abilities. As his mother, I have always been there to protect him, redirect him, and cover for him. I have worn myself threadbare reliving life through his choices. Now detaching with love happens. I watch him burn himself out in a safe place where he cannot hurt himself or others, much. For the first time in years I am not on red alert, and I begin to explore *his* and *ours* as separate entities, and work on *ours*.

We are part of a team advocating for our son, joined by men who love him as much as we do, and who will not let go. He is safe. We love the weekends when he can come home, and we watch him take ownership of his life and begin to change.

On Saturday nights when our family eats pizza, we watch an episode of our favorite show, an old black-and-white of hometown America. The ending always follows a pattern. A good closing act finishes the story, and the screen turns black, but quickly brightens again to tuck in one more scene, for humor or closure or beauty. Then the final black screen comes, and the credits. My younger children are not sure which is the real ending, and would like to watch more, so when the black screen comes or the time elapsed feels about right and the closing moment hangs poised, they shout hopefully, *Not the end! Not the end!*

In God we trust, and know that every ending we have seen so far is temporary.

I sit with a dear friend who is also a therapist. She comes to God in another way yet. She comes with friends, comes intending to bring body and soul together and to connect all the parts.

She is the first person who enables me to access the frozen place, to take a good long look at it and to be thankful for what it did, saving and protecting me until I could handle more. We look together at this part, and we talk through layers of circumstances to thoughts to feelings to feelings-about-feelings to expectations and all the way down to soul. It is hard and painful work. When I reach the last stop, the deepest, I find I am standing before Christ once again without protections, my heart turned inside out with longing. *Can you see him now?* she asks, and I can.

I kneel before him and I ask him the deepest yearning of my heart. I ask him to show me where he is. Where he is in the new homes of my various foster children, where he is at my son's camp, where he is in my house. I wait before him in the awful vulnerability of stating desire before another human, a place I cannot come alone. She holds him with one hand and me with the other. We watch my protections melting in unstoppable rivulets, and I feel myself to be what I am: completely undone and completely safe.

He shows me.

I have found him on the living room carpet of a friend. I have found him in the Lord's Supper. I have found him in the workplace of my mentor, in our habitual sharing and praying together. I have found him in the congregation where the babies smile and the prayers rise, my spirit lifted on the updraft. I have found him with my head on the breast of a mother, her arms tight around me while I drip all my tears down her neckline, while she says the name of Jesus over me, while her kiss is hearty on my cheek. I have found him in my home when my husband's hands are on my head. I have found him in the anointing oil and the songs of the saints. I have found him in the pagan and the holy. I have found him in the earth.

I have found him, and I take off my shoes.

This I have learned, after half a lifetime of trying to be the strong one who has the prayers to give for others who are in need. All who walk with Jesus need the prayers of others, and our talking with him about each other is best done in pairs: when I pray for you, you pray for me. I am not between you and him, nor you between him and me. We are the priesthood of believers, and we bring each other. You stand for me before him and I come on the strength of your faith. I ask your sins to be forgiven, and you take my hand and attend me to a Christ of whom we stand in need together.

It has taken me forever to learn that brokenness and need are the believer's intended posture.

That the cracks also are sacred.

That the scars on the hands of Jesus are holy flesh.

And that resurrection is always on the near horizon.

We watch the layers peel away from our son, his unhappiness falling from him first, replaced by the megawatt smile we've missed. He gains skills and experiences we could never give him, and earns confidence in those spaces. He learns respect and hard work. He develops friendships and honesty. His counselor chiefs walk him step by step, from being open about his negative choices to taking the call-outs of his peers and authorities in order to avoid those choices, to initiating healthy choices, to encouraging the positive choices of others on his team, and finally, to calling out others' negative choices and refusing to participate in or ignore them.

What I do for my foster children, my son's counselors do for him. Teaching new habits and a different style of living. Offering care and support and belonging. Becoming a trusted caregiver, tucking someone else's child into bed far from home, helping him through until he can return. We need what we give, and give what we need. In this we receive grace by the bucket.

My world is a scruffier place than it used to be, no longer a neat dichotomy. Every human in it has something to seek, and something to offer. Everyone who gives must receive from somewhere.

Our son graduates and comes home at last, with a party and honors and unmixed gratitude. At last we are one hundred percent certain the journey was worth it. Life is rich with four beloved children in our home. We imagine we are gliding into a smooth and rosy harbor, but of course that is not true. We will crack again, and again. Our people will be there for us. Out of the wreckage, redemption will grow.

Our family talks about wilderness camp with families who come asking about their own difficult sons. We tell them they will make it if they choose that path. We become passionate about foster care apart from adoption, an act of loving and losing that gives families a second chance, that sets them up for success. We will be doing this for a long time, God willing, signing up again and again. Scars that heal.

My faith has become one shot through with ongoing doubt. I long for the certainty I once had, of who I am as a good person and who God is as a good God, and of the easy path to finding peace with him. I measure us better now by what I know we are not.

I know he is not looking away. I know he is not weak. I know he is not detached and pristine and squeaky clean up there somewhere doling out judgments on the populace. I know he is not blamable, and not unkind. I know he is not afraid of my feelings, failures, and experiences. He does not need me to perform for him and make things work out, to be a triumph so that people will think highly of him. He is already highest. He is already good.

And he is not done. This I know for sure.

I know I am small and needy, but not abandoned. I am not in charge, not on the inside of all the divine wisdom and purpose. I am not invincible or independent, able to pull off a perfect life and all the things. I know he doesn't need my moving and acting and succeeding in the world nearly as much as he needs me. My hand in his.

One night when my soul is wildly unsettled, I lie by the shore of a lake and in desperation pour out my heart to him again. *It is not turning out. I must have done it all wrong. Who are you?* When I have said it all and am empty, the quiet begins to soak in. My fancy is captured by the smooth, still water, the starlight and the rushes, the joyful splashing of an otter who is fishing and dancing near the shore. Out of the silence the Father speaks to me in a tone he's never used before, reassuring, affectionate, almost playful. He says the worlds we move in are fluid to him, all things changing and easily moveable, buoyant in the waters of supreme love. He is not threatened by any of it. He is not worried that we will mess it up. He can arrange it all, guide the stars in the sky and the animals in the water and the people on this old earth. Nothing in my life has been outside of divine orchestration and redemption. He says if it wasn't part of the plan before, it surely is now. He will use it all.

He and his people have what I need. He is already preparing miraculous provision for what comes next.

He says, *Trust me, small one. All you have ever experienced is held in love. What would the world be like if pipsqueaks like you could mess up my plans? What kind of a God would I be?*

I do not see it yet, but I hold out my hands and know he is never wrong.

To be honest, from this side of the story I think it best to crack as early and as wide as we can, and let the grace in.

Not the End! Not the End!

Additional Resources

In this book, I touched on many topics that I do not have the time or the wisdom to adequately address. If you are looking for more input in a particular area, here are some resources I recommend.

EMOTIONAL HEALTH
Johann Hari. *Lost Connections: Why You're Depressed and How to Find Hope*. Bloomsbury, 2019.

Nadine Burke Harris. *The Deepest Well: Healing the Long-Term Effects of Childhood Adversity*. Mariner Books, 2018.

Stephen S. Ilardi. *The Depression Cure: The 6-Step Program to Beat Depression without Drugs*. Da Capo Lifelong Books, 2009.

FIREFIGHTING FAMILIES

Ellen Kirschman. *I Love a Fire Fighter: What the Family Needs to Know*. Guilford Press, 2004.

Lori Mercer. *Honor and Commitment: Standard Life Operating Guidelines for Firefighters and Their Families*. 24-7 Commitment, 2016.

FOSTER CARE

Mike Berry. *Confessions of an Adoptive Parent: Hope and Help from the Trenches of Foster Care and Adoption*. Harvest House, 2017.

Kathy Harrison. *Another Place at the Table*. Tarcher/Penguin, 2003.

Lynda Mullaly Hunt. *One for the Murphys*. Puffin Books, 2012.

Patrick McDonnell. *South*. Little, Brown, 2008.

LESS IS MORE

Tsh Oxenreider. *Organized Simplicity: The Clutter-Free Approach to Intentional Living*. Betterway Home Books, 2010.

Richard Swenson. *Margin: Restoring Emotional, Physical, Financial, and Time Reserves to Overloaded Lives*. NavPress, 2004.

MISCARRIAGE

Angie Smith. *I Will Carry You: The Sacred Dance of Grief and Joy*. B&H Books, 2010.

Kathe Wunnenberg. *Grieving the Child I Never Knew: A Devotional for Comfort in the Loss of Your Unborn or Newly Born Child*. Zondervan, 2015.

PARENTING

Rachel Jankovic. *Fit to Burst: Abundance, Mayhem, and the Joys of Motherhood*. Canon Press, 2013.

——— *Loving the Little Years: Motherhood in the Trenches*. Canon Press, 2010.

Madeline Levine. *The Price of Privilege: How Parental Pressure and Material Advantage Are Creating a Generation of Disconnected and Unhappy Kids*. Harper, 2008.

Thomas W. Phelan. *1-2-3 Magic: Effective Discipline for Children 2–12*. ParentMagic, 2003.

PARENTING CHILDREN WHO DON'T FIT THE MOLD

Rex Forehand and Nicholas Long. *Parenting the Strong-Willed Child: The Clinically Proven Five-Week Program for Parents of Two- to Six-Year-Olds*. McGraw Hill, 2002.

Emily Perl Kingsley. "Welcome to Holland" (essay). 1987.

Carol Stock Kranowitz. *The Out-of-Sync Child: Recognizing and Coping with Sensory Processing Disorder*. Perigee, 2005.

Miriam S. Lind. *No Crying He Makes*. Herald Press, 1972.

Lucy Jane Miller. *Sensational Kids: Hope and Help for Children with Sensory Processing Disorder*. G. P. Putnam's Sons, 2006.

Stanley Turecki and Leslie Tonner. *The Difficult Child*. Revised edition. Bantam Books, 2000.

PHYSICALITY

Tish Harrison Warren. *Liturgy of the Ordinary: Sacred Practices in Everyday Life*. InterVarsity Press, 2016.

PURITY AND BETRAYAL TRAUMA

Sheri Keffer. *Intimate Deception: Healing the Wounds of Sexual Betrayal*. Revell, 2018.

Heath Lambert. *Finally Free: Fighting for Purity with the Power of Grace*. Zondervan, 2013.

Vicki Tiede. *When Your Husband is Addicted to Pornography: Healing Your Wounded Heart*. New Growth Press, 2012.

RELATIONSHIPS

Dee Brestin. *The Friendships of Women: The Beauty and Power of God's Plan for Us*. Revised edition. David C Cook, 2008.

Emerson Eggerichs. *Love and Respect: The Love She Most Desires; The Respect He Desperately Needs*. Thomas Nelson, 2004.

Mike Mason. *The Mystery of Marriage*. 20th anniversary edition. Multnomah, 2005.

SPIRITUAL GROWTH AND HEALING

John Baillie. *A Diary of Private Prayer*. Revised edition. Touchstone, 1996.

Emily P. Freeman. *Grace for the Good Girl: Letting Go of the Try-Hard Life*. Revell, 2011.

Samuel Rutherford. *The Loveliness of Christ*. Revised edition. Banner of Truth, 2007.

James Bryan Smith. *The Good and Beautiful God: Falling in Love with the God Jesus Knows*. InterVarsity Press, 2009.

SUFFERING LOVE AND NONRESISTANCE

Bread and Wine: Readings for Lent and Easter. Plough, 2003.

Acknowledgments

I praise the supremacy and beauty of my Father, his son Jesus, and his Holy Spirit. I love you most and offer my halfpenny work to you, grateful for the way that you receive all of me—the honorable, the shameful, and the silly—and call me your own.

I respect my husband Ryan so much. Thank you for being one with me, and growing always deeper in joy and faithfulness and intimacy. You have never given up on me even when I've given up on myself. I wouldn't trade our story for anything. I love you.

I love my children, Aarick, Regan, Kelly, and Jenny, and the babies who have found their home on the breast of Christ. Thank you for granting me the ongoing privilege of being your mom—I have found great joy in life with you. Thank you for giving me the time and grace I needed to grow into a better mother than I used to be. I ask Jesus to help me become better still. Thanks for reading these stories I wrote, approving the ones that included you and telling me the ones you wanted left out. You are what I care about most in this world, and I believe in God's work in each of you.

I honor my parents, John and Barb Coblentz, who gave me the best of childhoods. Your care for me was more than enough, and I'm so grateful for you. I honor my parents-in-law, Cliff and Loila Zook, who gave me my husband. Thanks to all four of you for letting me talk about the pieces I needed to in this book. Your faithful love has been an anchor for me and mine, a generational heritage I am blessed to receive.

I gratefully acknowledge my siblings, John, Jean, Ben, Josh, Andy, and Ted (and your lovely spouses). Thanks for growing up with me, refusing to let me take myself too seriously even when I was bound and determined to do so, hashing out so many of life's issues in long conversations, and helping to shape me into who I am. You are the best.

I appreciate the many mothers who have taken me under their wing when I needed it. To my longtime mentor Irene, thank you for all the deep talks, and for teaching me about being honest and receiving grace. To Cynthia, Gladys, Marie, Sharon Y., Dorcus S., Rebecca S., and Dorcus H., along with my aunts, my grandmothers, and many more, thank you for coaching me through everything from baking wheat bread to letting go of shame to birthing a baby to washing crusty dishes to listening to the Holy Spirit to knowing how to grieve to taking ownership of my space in this world. Thank you for all the gifts. Thank you for praying over me.

I bless the girlfriends who have graced my life since day one. I'm afraid I will miss someone important if I start naming you, but how can I help it when you taught me all of chapter 6 and more? Thanks to Jo and Rachel and others for the parties, fights, and secrets when I was little. Plain City life-bringers— you know who you are. My beautiful friends Becca, Cris, and

Wendy for twenty-five years and counting of belonging and love. Kim and Chastin for lighting the way in loving a Zook man. Shaunda, my beautiful bestie, for everything—I have no words, just heart emojis. Carla for truth-telling and energy, Janelle for wisdom and precedent, Joann for presence and tenacity, Tina for humor and empathy, and literally dozens more of the dearest women for coffee talks, practical helps, and endless love. You have saved my sanity and expanded my world.

I thank sweet Anita and her mom, and my dear friend Heidi, for the dragon wings! and I thank Mr. George Washington Carver (or whoever was responsible) for all the peanut butter. I owe you big.

I salute the birth and adoptive families of our many foster children, who have taught me so much about love and being. Special thanks to Ashleigh and James and Leon and Kellen, who opened our hearts. Deep gratitude to Rod and Tina and Lilly and Lucy—thank you for doing what I could not. Joy to M&M and their competent mother A. Happiness to JBH and his precious family. There are more—I treasure you. Thank you for trusting me and forgiving my mistakes and letting me be part of your lives in lasting ways. My love forever to each child I called mine for a time.

I hail the professionals who guided me through deep waters. My great thanks to those who permitted me to quote them in this book—our foster agent Marie Schwartz (chapter 9), counselor Patrick Lashbrook (chapter 11), and friend and therapist Janelle Glick (chapter 12). You have added immeasurably to my family's resilience and courage.

I confess the faith of the people of God, especially those at Meadville Mennonite Chapel who have patiently loved us, forgiven us, and allowed us to be what we are: both whole and broken. Thank you for a place to belong, to forge faith, and to renew our spirits when we are weary. The past year has been incredibly hard, but we're going to make it.

I recognize the gift that the prayers of John Baillie have been to me in *A Diary of Private Prayer* (1936). In the prelude that begins chapter twelve, I am inspired by and gratefully acknowledge his work.

I give a shoutout to the lively, thoughtful, and fun-loving readers of my blog, *Confessions of a Woman Learning to Live*, who unabashedly praised and spanked me as needed over the past nine years. Thank you for believing in me and helping me grow as a writer and a person.

I celebrate the team at Herald Press and their associates, who were dazzlingly competent and kind. Thank you to Valerie Weaver-Zercher for connecting me here. Thank you to Amy Gingerich for your skillful team management. Thank you to Reuben Graham for the brilliant cover I love so much, and the beautiful design work. Thank you to Sara Versluis and Meghan Florian for your careful polishing of the details, and for your kindness in letting my voice stay my own. Thank you to the marketing team LeAnn Hamby, Joe Questel, and Alyssa Bennett Smith, for your gracious work and coaching behind the scenes. Thank you to the vibrant Margot Starbuck, who blew my theories and fears about editors to shreds and became such a gorgeous cheerleader.

All of you helped to create me, let alone this book, and I'm grateful.

The Author

Shari Zook is a pastor's wife, mother of four, and foster parent for the past seven years. She bakes cakes, grows herbs, and reads amazing books, but her heart is in raising children, crafting words, and connecting with women. She lives with her family in northwestern Pennsylvania and attends Meadville Menno-  nite Chapel, where her husband, Ryan, pastors. Her blog, *Confessions of a Woman Learning to Live*, can be found at sharizook.com.